UNDERCOOKED

UNDERCOOKED

How I Let

Food Become

My Life Navigator

and How Maybe

That's a Dumb

Way to Live

DAN AHDOOT

CROWN
NEW YORK

Copyright © 2023 by Dan Ahdoot

All rights reserved.

Published in the United States by Crown, an imprint of Random House, a division of Penguin Random House LLC, New York.

CROWN and the Crown colophon are registered trademarks of Penguin Random House LLC.

Library of Congress Cataloging-in-Publication Data
Names: Ahdoot, Dan, author.
Title: Undercooked / Dan Ahdoot.
Description: First edition. | New York: Crown, [2023]
Identifiers: LCCN 2022036804 (print) | LCCN 2022036805 (ebook) |
    ISBN 9780593240793 (hardcover) | ISBN 9780593240809 (ebook)
Subjects: LCSH: Ahdoot, Dan. | Gastronomy—United States. | Food—
    Psychological aspects. | Restaurateurs—United States—Biography.
Classification: LCC TX910.5.A29 A3 2023 (print) | LCC TX910.5.A29 (ebook) |
    DDC 647.95092 [B]—dc23/eng/20220817
LC record available at https://lccn.loc.gov/2022036804
LC ebook record available at https://lccn.loc.gov/2022036805

Printed in the United States of America on acid-free paper

crownpublishing.com

9 8 7 6 5 4 3 2 1

First Edition

Book design by Debbie Glasserman

I DEDICATE THIS BOOK TO MY BROTHER SOLLY.

CONTENTS

Introduction
ix

1
APPETIZER (JK)
3

2
A HUNTER WITH
A GATHERER VIBE
11

3
DAN THE
INTERN
21

4
MEDITATIONS ON
FALAFEL PHIL
37

5
UNDERCOOKED
56

6
ELK CAMP
71

7
HELLO MY NAME
IS MUMUN HELEN
108

8
CREAM
OF TARTAR
125

9
CHASING
DEAR
135

10
FORGETTING
IN PARIS
166

11
FEELS ON
WHEELS
182

Epilogue
205

Acknowledgments
217

INTRODUCTION*

I LIKE FOOD. A LOT. IT'S AN OBSESSION. AND I'M NOT JUST TALKING about how eating a good meal makes me happy. Which, don't get me wrong, it does. A good meal gives me more happiness than almost anything else in life, including sex, money, and sex. Food has had an outsize impact on my life—far more than it should in some cases. When you peel back all the layers of the Vidalia onion that is my life, many of the biggest moments reveal some sort of relationship to food. Food has made me a better brother and a worse son; it has given me the best of

---

*I was debating calling this introduction "Appetizer" or "Amuse-Bouche." But then I figured I'd have to commit to the menu thing for the whole book, and there would be dumb chapters called "Palate Cleansers" and "Cheese Course" and the end would be called "Check, Please" and that would be grating. Oh, also, get used to footnotes. They're my love language.

friends and the worst of enemies. It's made me stay in bad relationships longer than I should have, and it's made me exit great relationships because of dietary restrictions. Food has taken me all over the world and helped make my dining room a destination. It has turned me into a gun owner, an animal rights activist, an arsonist,* and a restaurateur. When most people say they have an unhealthy relationship with food, they mean they eat too much of it or too little. When I say I have an unhealthy relationship with food, I mean it's what gives my life meaning. That's a really dumb way to live your life, as the stories in this book will prove.

So why should you read this book? Good question. I mean, I'm a comedian, but there are definitely funnier books out there. And I love food, but there are better food memoirs on the shelves. Before you print out your Amazon return label, let me say this: I'm probably the best comedian in the country with a deep obsession with food, so that's something, right? I think? Okay, maybe print the label, but keep it in a drawer for now.†

I have two fridges in my garage. One is a wine fridge full of bottles from across the world that I have accumulated over the last couple of decades with help from my connections in the upscale restaurant world. And next to it is a deep freezer full of meat from the animals I've hunted and butchered. I like looking at these two fridges side by side, because they're pretty telling of who I am, my bougie side and my country side proudly on display, powered by the same electrical outlet. But the road

---

*Allegedly. Shout-out to Crown Publishing's legal department!
†And to those of you who bought this book at an independent mom-and-pop bookshop, thank you! Also, I hope your grandkids are checking in often.

to filling these two fridges was not easy and, a lot of times, was gut-wrenchingly unpleasant.

Letting your stomach be your guide through life is probably one of our most misunderstood fantasies. We enviously watch food shows where Phil Rosenthal and Padma Lakshmi and David Chang travel the world taking happy bites while beaming for the camera, desperately trying to come up with different ways to say "This is so good."* We all wish we could have that job. And yet, the person who invented the genre, my idol Anthony Bourdain, died by suicide. I'm not saying that being a globe-trotting foodie who went to the ends of the earth and ate at the best restaurants was what killed him, but it sure as hell didn't save him.

Okay, shit's getting dark. Let me bring it back. I once had to vigorously wash my dick in a taco truck sink in San Miguel de Allende, Mexico, because I touched raw jalapeños and then took a piss. We back? Good. Also, if you're reading this, sorry, Mrs. Jimenez.

Unfortunately, knowing that food is an unreliable life navigator isn't enough to make me quit my reliance on its busted compass. I'm in too deep. That in itself should be enough to make this book entertaining. The second-most-translated book in the world is *Don Quixote,* the story of a guy who can't find his way because he is completely delusional. "Dan" is close enough to "Don," so have fun at my quixotic expense. Oh, by the way, the most translated book in the world? The Bible. I've never read it. Too many dietary restrictions.

---

*If I hear Chang say "This is fucking delicious" one more time, I'm burning down every Momofuku on the planet. Don't worry if you don't get the reference; there's still a ton in this book for you.

UNDERCOOKED

1

APPETIZER
(JK)

I GREW UP ONE OF THREE BOYS. MY OLDER BROTHER, SOLLY, WAS AN amazing athlete; my younger brother, David, was charming, cute, and got all the attention. I had a nondescript, chubby vibe, and like most middle children was forced to create new ways to get attention. Because my father was born in Iran and spent his formative years in Switzerland as a student, he had a robust passion for food. He did his best to pass down his European trappings to us. He raised us speaking French, drinking wine before our Bar Mitzvahs, and eating stinky illegal unpasteurized cheeses he would smuggle into the States. But neither of my brothers shared his love for "la gourmandise," as he'd call it. I (chubby vibe) did.

I'm not sure if I actually loved the eating, or loved what it got me, an opportunity to bond with him on something my brothers could not. Either way, chicken or egg, as a child I developed an appreciation for both a perfectly roasted chicken and a sublimely poached egg. I was a finicky foodie in the making. By age eight, I knew which dishes demanded which fork, and I never got ice cream on my face when eating from even the drippiest of cones. When I turned nine, my parents took me to a Long Island pizza joint. When we entered, I looked at them and said, "It's my birthday, and you're taking me out for pizza?" My dad still tells that story with pride.*

My dad and I would go to restaurants alone together. While my mom stayed at home with my brothers, he and I would set out on culinary adventures in New York City. And like most adventures, our dining escapades required a uniform. I would don my restaurant blazer—an olive-green wool number with brown suede elbow patches—over one of Solly's hand-me-down shirts that had a stain on the breast pocket, which my blazer just covered. When I was seated, chunks of flab would gasp for air between the buttons. My khakis had two pleats, because I wasn't fucking around. My dad, in a handsome suit, helped me tie the laces on my moccasins, and we were off.

Those trips are my fondest memories as a kid because I was finally able to enjoy my dad's attention without having to compete for it. We reveled in the most avant-garde foods New York City had to offer. Fresh pastas at Mezzaluna, impeccable

---

*No offense to Gino's of Great Neck. You guys are still the first place I hit up when I visit my parents. I've gotten slightly less pretentious than I was at nine.

côte de boeuf at Les Halles. For my eleventh birthday, Dad took me to Le Cirque. Let me repeat. We went to a *New York Times* three-star restaurant for my eleventh birthday. Quite an upgrade from Gino's.* And I can still recite the menu from memory. There was something called a Trio, a holy trinity of caviar, smoked salmon, and foie gras. A silky butternut squash soup with huckleberries. A seared Alaskan black cod that melted in my mouth. Then something I had never had before—duck confit. A duck that was cooked in its own fat. The crispy skin and lusciously gamy, unctuous flesh beneath it didn't just create a memory—that memory was nailed, à la Martin Luther, to the door of my brain.

Having this special connection with my dad helped me to be less contentious with Solly and David. I had textbook middle child syndrome—I could've written the foreword to said textbook. But because I knew that I had a piece of my dad they'd never get, I was able to let down my guard and become a better brother. My being a better brother to them allowed them to be better brothers to me. Solly and I became best friends. He was my cheerleader, my mentor, my idol. I was a decent piano player, so he convinced me I could be a pro. I was not great at tennis, yet he told me that if I kept practicing, I could be, like him, number one on the college team. He gave me the confidence that helped me eventually become a comedian. (You don't try to become a professional comedian without a healthy dose of delusion.)

When I was sixteen, and he was twenty, we hit our sweet

---

*Again, I really love you guys.

spot. I was having a tough time adjusting in high school because I was weird and eccentric.* So I'd go visit Solly at
Brandeis to get away. He showed me that weird and eccentric
were actually valuable assets at university, and that if I applied
myself in high school, there was light at the end of the tunnel.
He was right. He saw in me a potential that nobody else did.
And my fondness for his wisdom was at its peak. Sadly, it
would last only six months longer. He got cancer and died. Out
of nowhere. Fast, cruel, devastating.

My parents became zombies of their former selves and
eventually took a sharp turn into religion. I veered in the opposite direction. We'd been raised pretty lax Jews, but suddenly, they became true believers. While they were saying,
"This is all God's plan," I was insisting, "If God existed, Solly
wouldn't be dead." I would try to debate them, but as soon as
cracks started to form in their arguments, they would bubble
with anger and anxiety. Then I'd scream, "Why can't we just
have a normal conversation about this?" and I'd storm out. I
realize now that the reason we couldn't have a normal conversation about this was because if I won the argument, the after-
life was a myth and they'd never see their firstborn again.

With religion came kosher laws. And kosher laws killed dining out—at least in the places we used to go. The top echelon of
NYC restaurants was replaced with subpar kosher immigrant
eateries in Forest Hills, Queens, with fluorescent lighting, sticky
menus, and the smell of ferment. We frequented restaurants
whose only raison d'être was that they served the right kinds of

---

* I had a fucking restaurant uniform, guys.

meat on the right kinds of plates. Le Cirque, only a couple of miles away, inhabited another universe.

The day my brother died, I also lost the only meaningful connection I had with my dad. My love of food suddenly became an obsession, to fill in the hole my dad used to occupy. The goal was no longer about seeking out great restaurants; now it was about chasing an impossible high. But that didn't stop me from trying.

After college, I moved to New York City. I was an open-mic comic, not making much money, and every penny I saved went to food gods: April Bloomfield, Mario Batali,* Wylie Dufresne, Gabrielle Hamilton, Dan Barber, and Keith McNally. My parents had Yahweh; I had Anthony Bourdain. I ate pork and shellfish for the first time. I had never craved pork or shellfish, nor had I wondered how they tasted. The smell of bacon held no hypnotic powers over me, as it does for most people. It was not happily that I ate these things; I forced myself to. They did not go down easily. They had to push past tons of pain and shame gagging in the other direction. Each piece of treif † pumped guilt into my veins. The more foreign a dish was, the more wrong it felt, with virgin sensations bombarding my palate—the slick yet sticky viscosity of pork fat, the cartilaginous give of octopus, the slimy loogie-ness of oysters. Guilt be damned, these were textures my father would *never* feel, and I could start holding that over him. Not only did I get over the prohibition and then an aversion to these foods, but I actually

---

*I know. More on that later.
†"Treif" is a Yiddish word that basically means nonkosher food. See, Mom! I retained something from Hebrew school.

started to crave them. Like moths to a mesmerizing flame, my eyes homed in on the word "charcuterie" on menus. Sea urchin wasn't just a delicacy, it was a way of telling my dad, "You don't want to eat with me? No worries. I wouldn't be able to eat with you anyway!"

But eating the best foods in the world wasn't enough to fill the hole, I needed to *make* them. Making what I ate would let me literally feed the hole. I was pretty well connected in the NYC restaurant scene by then, and friends pulled strings to get me a gig as a kitchen intern at the Michelin one-star establishment—ironically named for a rebellious Jew to work at—the Spotted Pig. I learned how to make some of the most delicious items ever: chicken liver toast drenched in port and Madeira on crusty bread—a hearty, medieval-looking dish that could've been a passed appetizer at the Red Wedding. A haddock chowder whose mere whiff makes anything Herman Melville wrote seem landbound. And gnudi, pillowy ricotta dumplings with crispy sage and brown butter sauce, a dish so mind-altering it could make MDMA exclaim, "Hey gnudi, how the hell did you do that?"

I read food books for pleasure—not just cookbooks, but food memoirs too. *Comfort Me with Apples* by Ruth Reichl, *A Year in Provence* by Peter Mayle, and, of course, Bourdain's *Kitchen Confidential*. I felt like I belonged to a club of cool people who understood me better than my own family did. But I still wasn't full. There needed to be more, a frontier of food that I hadn't yet explored. Something both fulfilling and rebellious. Something like hunting.

This was way before Michael Pollan and *The Omnivore's*

Dilemma made it hip to hunt. Before Joe Rogan was posting pics of himself on Instagram with a dead elk and the caption "Fuck yeah, I smoked this thing from 40 yards with my bow and I'm going to eat it raw!" At least in my part of the world, hunting was considered a disgusting pastime reserved for cousin fuckers in serious need of dental work.* But this Jew from Long Island with perfect teeth wanted in, for all the wrong reasons. Killing and guns were not things I grew up with, and the thought of hunting was revolting. However, the fact that something food related would be so anathema to my dad's constitution was indeed enticing. You couldn't really beat the trifecta of killing a nonkosher animal with a gun.

I never went to therapy after my brother died, so becoming a foodie and a hunter were my poor ways of surviving. And coming to that realization, while profound, doesn't mean I need to abandon my emotional crutches. Tiger Woods became Tiger Woods because his dad put him through intense psychological training when he was a little boy. Does he know that? Yes. Is he thrilled to be golf's GOAT? Of course. I think. I haven't seen the latest documentary. I still crave new restaurants, cuisines, food adventures. Sure, my food adventurism has on occasion led me astray, but it has also given me great friends, epic meals around the world I will never forget, and more bliss than anything else in my life.† And believe it or not, I didn't stop hunting either.

---

*Or dentists in need of mental work. RIP, Cecil the lion.
†Okay, I know this is a more rosy picture of my food adventurism than I gave in the introduction, but I'm honestly conflicted. If the painstaking process of writing this book eventually gives me a definitive answer, I'll delete this footnote.

Just as with eating pork and shellfish, which I now love, I forced myself to keep at hunting. Eventually, the killing became easier, which made the adventure more fun and gave me access to foods I could never buy in a store* and people I would never otherwise break bread with.† And though the hunting and gathering both arose from a sixteen-year-old kid's longing for relationships he'd never get back, they're still my favorite things to do in life.

---

*There's nothing more local, organic, or free-range than a deer who lived a wonderful life and had a real bad last five seconds.
†That's right! Some of those guys with awful teeth became my best friends! And they all have a great sense of humor so I can write this about them. Right? Guys? Hello?

2

A HUNTER
WITH A
GATHERER VIBE

WHEN I DECIDED TO EXPLORE THE WORLD OF HUNTING, I DIDN'T HAVE
to look too far. I just called Mo. Mo is my alpha male best friend
from college, and an avid hunter. However, he didn't get into
the pastime because he read Michael Pollan and wanted to ex-
pand his ethical horizons. Mo's just a meat-and-potatoes redneck hunter. In fact, the name "Mo" and "redneck hunter" go
well together. But in this case, Mo is short for Mohaned. He is
an Iraqi Muslim, and I'm an Iranian Jew. Yet we were going to
put aside all the millennia-spanning religious and political dif-
ferences to fuck up some poor animal.

Mo grew up in a little town in upstate New York called
Olean. Olean is about as red as you can get in New York.
MAGA hats aplenty, snake flags expressing fear of being trod-
den on, bumper stickers of AR-15s with the phrase "Gun Con-

trol Means Hitting Your Target." In some way it's even more red than red states. I've seen Confederate flags in Olean. Gross to see in the South, but more sinister to see in the North. So how did a first-generation Iraqi American grow up in a town an hour and a half south of Buffalo? His father, Adil, made a real tough decision fifty years prior.

Adil grew up in Baghdad, the son of a tailor, and decided to follow in his father's footsteps . . . sort of. He ended up sewing humans rather than clothes. Adil became a surgeon. As one of the better students in Baghdad, he qualified for a surgical residency in the United States. His plan was to ultimately return to the country he loved and share his newfound skills. However, Saddam's Baath Party quickly seized power, and Adil's father urged him to stay in America and start a life there.

Suddenly all alone, he tried to start his medical career in a big city with a sizable Muslim population, but the only offer came from a tiny hospital in a rural burg in western New York. Adil wasn't just far from his family and homeland; he was now the only Muslim in town.

He didn't experience too much intolerance; however, there was a brief moment of tension between him and the hospital's pathologist, Dr. Leo Moss. Leo was one of the only Jews in Olean, and he eyed the newbie from the Near East suspiciously, until one day when Adil delicately corrected a misdiagnosis of Leo's that could have had grave consequences for the patient. Leo thanked Adil by giving him a cake his wife was famous for. "I forget the name of this cake," Adil says, struggling to remember. "It was with chocolate and poppy seed. I loved it so much I made Mrs. Moss make me one every year. We became great friends." Babka diplomacy. What could be better?

Adil became a pillar of a community that never could have imagined its Samaritan being an Arab Muslim from Iraq. For many, Adil was the first Muslim they had ever met, and the person whose skills gave them the best odds of life over death. Ultimately, he helped build a mosque in town, moonlighted as a teacher of Arabic at the local college, and eventually donated the men's locker room at the YMCA. Let that sink in. The men's locker room at the Young Men's Christian Association in Olean, New York, is the Adil Al-Humadi Men's Locker Room. Adil is the epitome of the American dream and a perfect ambassador for Islam.

But starting a family in Olean meant having your children grow up around and possibly adopt the regional customs. And if there was ever a question about nature versus nurture, Mo has answered it with zero room for doubt. Nurture all the way.

Mo chews tobacco, plays ice hockey, and listens to nineties grunge in his pickup truck. Though he was raised Muslim, he became a fervent disciple of the local religion—hunting. But he was very different from the hunter I wanted to become— thoughtful, ethical, decked out in the finest Scottish tweed— one who hunts as a philosophical exercise in what it means to be fundamentally human. Not Mo. Mo killed animals with a certain bro'd-up glee that has always been hard for me to stomach. He had framed pictures of himself next to torqued dead animals, a childish grin on his giddy face. His raw enthusiasm made me queasy.

But he was the only hunter I knew, so I couldn't be choosy about my guide. And although we're the same age, Mo has always felt like an older brother to me. I'm goofy; he's serious. I'm lanky; he's burly. I'm all over the place; he's focused. He's

the firstborn in his family, and when I crave older-brother energy, he gives it to me. With that comes the desire younger
brothers have to impress older siblings. Mo was *very* surprised
that I wanted to try hunting. In his defense, I give off way
more of a gatherer vibe. His respect egged me on until there
was no turning back from my whim.

For my first hunt, we were going after ducks. How fitting.
Duck was my favorite food, my first real food memory, and
something my father took away when he went kosher. I was
going to make duck confit, from as scratch as it gets, and eat it
without him.

In the winter of early 2002, we began our quest on Long
Island. I had zero hunting clothing in my wardrobe,* so Mo
kitted me out with his gear. I am five foot seven, 150 pounds.
Mo is six foot one, 220 pounds. Hunting clothes are baggy as is,
because the words "hunting" and "tapered" don't live in the
same world. I looked like someone who had stapled his stomach a year ago and was showing off how drastically small he
had become by wearing his old clothes.† We got up super early,
carried our canoe to the frigid waters of Long Island Sound,
and paddled past residential areas, wearing full camo with
guns and ammo. Two brown dudes, *very* shortly after 9/11.

In fact, somebody called the fish and game warden on us,
which would normally be fine, except that I forgot my hunting
license at home—I used Mo's Dad's.‡ When we got stopped by
the game warden, I put on a fake Arab accent, pretending to be
Adil Al-Humadi. Yup. Months after 9/11, when Middle East-

---

*Shocker.
†I would make a Jared from Subway reference here, but . . . you know.
‡Allegedly. I got you, legal team.

ern people were frantic to pass as Latino, I, a Jew, faked being an Arab Muslim to deal with the authorities.*

Hunting on Long Island differs from hunting in most parts of the United States. Usually, hunting is a solitary pastime that takes place deep in the recesses of nature, away from the modern world, where man can tap into his most primal, prehistoric instincts. Not on Long Island. When we found our spot, hidden among the reeds of a sandbar, we could still see houses and boats, and hear cars screaming down the Long Island Expressway. Nothing kills the mood of a solitary hunt like the muffled sound of an ice cream truck in the distance.

We set up decoys, and Mo called in a duck. Side note about duck hunting: It's pretty messed up. I know you might think hunting in general is wrong, but duck hunting is especially so. Ducks travel in a crew.† They're social animals. However, there are always a couple of rejects who can't keep up, or don't fit in, and they live a loner life—*that's the duck you're hunting for!* Let's call him Myron. You set up decoys in the water and do a duck call that loosely translates as "Hey, Myron! Come hang! We have PlayStation here! It's super chill!" Then poor Myron, who just wants friends, flies over, stoked to finally be accepted, and you *drop* him. *Very* different from most other hunting. Most hunting is about sex. You kill a horny alpha dude who just wants to fuck. When you go turkey hunting, the turkey call sounds like "Oh, Mr. Turkey, I got some juicy

---

*Adil has a very fun Arab accent. I had a lot of practice imitating it because he got such a kick out of hearing me do it. It came in handy later in my career in ways I could never have imagined: Falafel Phil's voice (see Chapter 4) is an amped-up version of Adil's.

†Yup, that's the official term. (By the way, a hunting buddy reading my chapter called me frantically to tell me it's a flock, not a crew. Hunters don't get sarcasm.)

breasts that could use some gobbling up." And then the frat boy alpha turkey struts in, all "Where's them turkey titties? I heard there's some turkey titties up in here!" *Boom!* Happy Thanksgiving.

Back to the hunt. A duck flew in toward us. I stood up, aimed, closed my eyes, and shot. Somehow, someway, I hit Myron. And I was ecstatic! I jumped up and down in my duvet of a hunting outfit, hugging Mo and screaming at the top of my lungs—maybe because the hunter/gatherer part of my brain that had been dormant for my entire life was suddenly awake. Well, Duvet Crockett went back to sleep pretty quickly after I saw what I had done. I shot Myron out of the air, thinking he would die instantly, like in the Nintendo game *Duck Hunt*. But alas, he was still quite alive; I had only winged him.*
He struggled in the water, staring at me, knowing I was the cause of his misfortune, trying desperately to flee. So I shot him again, and his head and neck slumped over his body. We paddled out to him, and I picked him up out of the water, tears running down my face, while Mo was yelling and screaming, "Nice fucking shot, bro!" It wasn't a nice shot, and Mo was just trying to make me feel better. I pulled the mess of duck out of the water and felt its neck pulsate. I dropped the flesh and feathers in the boat. "Oh my god! He's still alive!" "Ah, don't worry about it," Mo said, as he grabbed Myron and gave his neck a couple of good yanks with the nonchalance of a bored cartoon cop twirling a baton. "WHAT THE FUCK?" "Dude, relax." "Relax? You just killed the thing with a yank!" "Yeah, because YOU couldn't with your gun." That shut me up.

---

*Shot him in the wing. Don't worry, I didn't know what that meant either.

After Mo bagged a duck of his own, we went home. In the basement, he laid the duck on its back, stepped on its wings, and pulled the breasts out. It's the easiest way to breast out a duck, and you get two nice pieces of meat. However, you lose the legs, the thighs, and, more important, the skin. What's the point of cooking duck if there's no skin? So as Mo was upstairs drinking post-hunt beers, I sat alone in his basement, defeathered Myron, gutted him, and slowly saw this poor thing I had maimed, then killed, turn into something you would buy at a supermarket. Along with the flesh, I brought back a sensory experience that I hadn't gone hunting for: the sight of the injured duck staring me in the face, the smell of shit and guts when I cleaned him, feathers sticking to the blood on my boots, duck skin pocked with shotgun pellets—these smells and images would flash-bomb my brain without warning months after the hunt.

Duck confit is a recipe that was born out of necessity. Before refrigeration, the French realized they could preserve meat longer when it was braised and stored in its own fat. Bonus— it's fucking delicious.* I had all the proper herbs and spices to confit my duck. However, when I got home, I needed a break from the madness, so I put Myron in the freezer, and there he stayed for days, then weeks, then months. Finally, I was cleaning my apartment, and when I came to the freezer, I decided it was time to cook my duck. As I began to score the skin and the flesh thawed, so did my memories of that day. The duck aromas threw me right back into Mo's basement, where I'd sat on the floor in a constant state of nausea.

---

*Ugh. We're all David Chang now.

I heated the duck fat, put in the legs, and the searing suddenly turbocharged the dull stench of that memory into my nostrils and mainlined it to my brain. I gagged, turned off the heat, took out a garbage bag, hurled the contents of the frying pan into it, and tossed in the rest of the raw meat. I wanted it out of my apartment and out of my life. I thought it would be too much of an affront to this already tainted experience for Myron's story to end in a grim trash chute of a Manhattan apartment building. So I threw on my jacket and headed out. Next thing I knew, I was overlooking the Hudson River with a bag of raw Myron in my hand. If I wasn't going to eat him, some bottom-feeder had to.

With a most unpoetic thud, I returned the duck to the water from which I had once reluctantly pulled him—trying at the very least to extract a weak excuse of symbolism to make up for my cowardice at not being able to eat what I had killed. As I watched the pieces sink to the watery floor, I was overtaken by the emotion of what an epic failure my coping mechanisms had been. Being a foodie, and now being a hunter, didn't change anything. It didn't make me appreciate meat more; it didn't make me feel cool in the eyes of Mo. His adoration was a sorry stand-in for the adoration I craved from my actual brother. It didn't bring back those cherished restaurant moments with my dad, and nothing was going to bring Solly back to me.

But I still saw hunting as a noble endeavor. And if the Nazis could get used to mass murder, I could get used to hunting.*

*Worst endorsement of hunting *ever*.

One of the best parts of hunting is that it's allowed me to strad-
dle two worlds that don't normally commingle. I have best
friends who are Trumpy NRA nuts who can't understand the
cultural milieu I come from, and are probably snickering right
now that I used the word "milieu." I've been able to open their
eyes way more effectively than a heavy-handed liberal not used
to this world ever could. A few of them are now on board with
gay marriage, and I even convinced one to get vaxxed!

Likewise, I'm a nonthreatening conduit for my latte-
drinking liberal friends* to ask all they want about the other
side and get insights into the vital role guns play for some people. The answer is not as easy as "let's just make all guns illegal." In fact, I've helped a lot of lefty friends buy guns of their
own. I always get the same phone call. "Dan, we *never* had this
conversation, but hypothetically, if someone wanted to get a
gun for home defense, what should she get?"

Hunting has also bonded me for life with Mo. Our upbring-
ings would not have set us up to be friends, but we're pretty
much inseparable. When my older brother died, as the middle
child I was suddenly thrust into the role of older brother to my
little brother, David. I wasn't good at it. I mean, it's not like the
understudy taking over the lead—it's the usher suiting up for
the role. Mo's advice was and still is vital in teaching me how
to be a solid older brother to David. That guidance makes him

---

*I *hate* the expression "latte liberals." How the poor latte got dragged into this whole par-
tisan mess might be the biggest casualty of our fractured politics. What is it about foaming
milk before mixing it in coffee that makes me out of touch? No, seriously. Email me your
answers at iheartlattes647@gmail.com. If I don't respond right away, I'm probably on my
yacht in Saint Barts. The wifi can be spotty. #IslandLife

more than a best friend. He's a godsend. And the fact that I'm Jewish and he's Muslim is such a nonissue that writing this sentence represents the most thought I've given it in years.

However, religion has allowed Mo to have a budding friendship with my father. Just as I'm not the best Jew, Mo isn't the best Muslim. He's become quite the oenophile, and has amassed an incredible collection of wines that, regretfully, he can never share with his father, a practicing Muslim. My dad, however, loves wine devoutly. So whenever Mo comes to Long Island, he visits my parents to enjoy an amazing bottle of wine with my all-too-eager father. Babka diplomacy has been replaced with Bordeaux diplomacy.

Mo's diplomacy doesn't end there. He followed in his family's footsteps and also became a tailor of sorts. He's an exceptional orthopedic surgeon. And unlike his father, he had his pick as to where he wanted to practice. Yet this Johns Hopkins–educated doctor chose to go back to his hometown and fill the hole left by Adil's retirement, and now he too is a pillar of the community—giving back to a place that's given him so much.

I go to Olean once a year for the opening of deer season. It's become a tradition. And when Mo and I go to the gym at the YMCA there, full of the whitest white people in the country, I stare at the baffling plaque that reads THE DR. ADIL AL-HUMADI MEN'S LOCKER ROOM. If it wasn't for that man blazing a bizarre trail from Baghdad to Buffalo, I'd have a much less rich life.

3

DAN THE INTERN

WHEN I GRADUATED FROM COLLEGE, I MOVED TO NEW YORK CITY TO be a stand-up comic. That's a sentence that haunts my immigrant parents to this day. They escaped oppression in Iran to give us a better chance at life. I went to Johns Hopkins University, graduated with honors, got into medical school, and then decided to throw it all away to be an open-mic comic. Instead of attending medical school at Cornell, I handed out comedy-show flyers on the sidewalk in exchange for three minutes of stage time at one o'clock in the morning on a Tuesday. Take *that,* Khomeini!

It was the early 2000s and a culinary renaissance was captivating the city. The words "casual fine dining" were suddenly pantry staples in the culinary lexicon and it was all because of one man—Mario Batali. Mario was doing something nobody had ever done before—with both food and dining. He was introducing the idea of eating locally, even with classic dishes from faraway lands. For example, if you're making a traditional branzino acqua pazza,* but rockfish, a maligned local fish, is of better quality than the branzino, *always* use the rockfish. In addition, he was serving dishes at a bar counter that rivaled some of the best fine dining the city had to offer, with Radiohead playing just slightly louder than expected in a restaurant setting. Dishes this good were never before enjoyed while tapping your feet to a beat. In fact, in his *New York Times* review of Mario's flagship restaurant, Babbo, Frank Bruni said he could only give three stars instead of four because the music didn't match the food—an error that would never happen today.

I knew of Mario way before Babbo. His show on the Food Network, *Molto Mario,* was hands down my favorite TV show. Not favorite cooking show, favorite of all TV. Better than *Seinfeld,* better than *Friends.* In college, I would fight with my roommates to turn off the game because Mario was on.† He was the best teacher and an amazing host. He'd bring three of his famous friends on his show to watch him cook, he'd answer their questions, then feed them amazing food that he had just whipped up in front of them. His celebrity buds, actors and musicians, normally the center of attention, were like wide-

---

*Incidentally, this is my favorite way to cook fish. Literally means "crazy water" in Italian and it's crazy simple. Put a whole fish in a pan large enough for it to fit inside, pour in enough water to cover the bottom, add some white wine, garlic, olive oil, cherry tomatoes, olives if you've got 'em, and whatever else might taste fun (scallions, mushrooms, herbs, the world is your oyster!—but probably don't add oysters). Cover, simmer, and in ten minutes you have an awesome fish in a delightful broth that is the perfect sauce.
†This was before DVR and streaming. I'm old.

eyed puppy dogs. It was mesmerizing. He was charming, talented, badass. I was socially awkward in college* and didn't have a lot of friends. I loved to cook, but that wasn't high social currency in a school where beer pong skills got you more high fives than homemade lasagna. I saw in Mario, for the first time, the cool that cooking could be. He was my idol.

The first time I went to Babbo was with Kayvan. Kayvan was my wealthy older cousin living the bachelor life in New York City while I was a new open mic-er. But he knew how much I loved Batali, so he took me, knowing full well I couldn't afford what we were ordering. Great guy.†

At Babbo I had my first Negroni, still my favorite cocktail twenty years later. The bitter flavor with little to balance in the way of sweetness was a perfect intro to Batali's dishes, which could best be described as balanced in the most unbalanced way. I had an appetizer that has become my Death Row Meal—warm lamb's tongue in a black truffle vinaigrette with pecorino and a three-minute egg. I loved how unassuming it was. This is not a pretty dish. Slices of braised lamb's tongue the size of dimes are interspersed with rags of roasted chante-

---

*Not anymore. I'm totes cool now. That's how cool people say "totally." Oh, it's not anymore? Damn it!

†It was Kayvan who told me my older brother had died, and then he filled in for Solly when I was in my twenties. However, if Solly was the angel on my shoulder, Kayvan was the devil—in the best possible way. Solly taught me how to serve a tennis ball, shoot a basketball, and finish my homework on time. Kayvan gave me my first bite of pork, my first hit of opium, and helped give me confidence in talking to women. He also passed on a handful of Kayvanisms—insights he amassed over his many years of Kayvan-ing. Imagine this wisdom conveyed in an accent not quite Persian, not quite American—something in between, maybe from a place called Ambiguoustan: "Bro, you see a girl you like at the bar, you buy two shots of tequila. One for you, and one for her. If she drinks the tequila, she parties. If she doesn't, you'd be wasting your time, and, silver lining, you'd have two shots of tequila."

relle mushrooms in a gray-tan mess. A poked poached egg lies on top, allowing the yolk to ooze over everything. You don't see the black truffles, but their perfume envelops you as soon as the plate drops. Again, the balance is off. It's soft on soft on soft. No breadcrumbs or crispy Parmesan to contrast textures. I took one bite and it smacked my eyes shut. While the mouthfeel and colors are soft and bland, they highlight the mindblowing flavors—woody chanterelles, funky anchovy in the sauce, defiant yet subtle offal flavor from the tongue, all tied with a black truffle bow. It was the most mature dish I had ever tasted. Understated in some ways, aggressive in others, it was masterful.

The entrée was Mario's famous beef cheek ravioli. In a city flush with basic red sauce/Alfredo joints, here was a dish that seemed teleported from the most regal of Roman osterias. Sturdy beef cheeks unclenched after an hours-long braise in Amarone, a powerful, jammy Italian red. The resulting meaty treasure was swaddled in translucent rags of freshly rolled pasta, joined together delicately, like prayer hands, and then kissed with a sauce of silky squab liver purée with anchovies and capers. You know when something is so good, it leaves you confused? Yeah.

Dessert was a magical saffron panna cotta that coated and comforted my tongue like a dairy cashmere sweater, leaving wisps of the Orient in its wake. But the real treat was Mario Batali himself walking through the dining room as Kayvan graciously paid the check. Batali came out quickly to greet a friend, and heads turned instantly as he marched by. He was portly and powerful. He wore his crisp double-breasted chef's jacket buttoned to the throat, pristinely white, no stains at all, because Mario don't spill nothing. His thick mane of chestnut hair was tied in his iconic ponytail, and his orange Crocs lit the room the way a shiny pair of Louboutins never could. He walked with purpose, a slight smile, head up, chest out. All eyes followed him furtively. He had the best restaurant in New York City, and he knew it. I was completely starstruck, and unlike everyone else there, I did *not* play it cool. My mouth was agape as he walked by us, and he noticed. I couldn't look away; I was hypnotized by this orange stallion. Probably, I guess, to make sure I wasn't having a stroke, he put his hand on my shoulder and said, "How is everything?" "Oh . . . my god. Mario. Um, it's like, so best." So best? He played it cool, though. "So best! What's better than so best, right? Nothing." He squeezed my shoulder and disappeared, leaving behind a whiff of fresh cut garlic, herbs, and starch—of both pasta and crisp dry cleaning. I melted in my chair. I bought* *The Babbo Cookbook* that night and spent much of the next decade treating it like my bible—studying, striving, perfecting.† Mario was my everything. I spent my free time cooking his recipes, watching him on TV, and saving up for my next meal.

In the new flush of my stand-up career, I was the highest-booked college comedian in the nation from 2006 to 2009. I performed at more than 165 colleges a year and was zigzagging the country just about every day. Though this might sound glamorous, it was anything but. Yes, some of the shows

---

*Kayvan bought me.
†While most of my cookbooks look pristine and decorative, this one looks like it fought in the Battle of Verdun.

were packed audiences in beautiful auditoriums, but those were outliers. The majority of the gigs were in awful settings— one, at Johnson & Wales in Charlotte, North Carolina, was outside on the quad of a school that had a train track crossing through it, and every fifteen minutes, my bits were, ahem, rail- roaded by a caboose chugging along. Another was in the cafe- teria of the University of Delaware, where every punch line was crushed by the roar of a smoothie stand's blender. The show at Everett Community College in Washington state was in a hallway. A hallway! Sans stage or microphone, like some lunatic feverishly proselytizing about the end of days, I yelled comedy at students at one in the afternoon as they shuffled from class to class.

After my first year of this grueling schedule, I decided to take a break. I needed something completely different, so I de- cided to take cooking classes at the French Culinary Institute in Manhattan. I discussed my plan with my buddy Tim, the manager of my neighborhood haunt, the much-lauded Spot- ted Pig. The chef was a young dynamo from England named April Bloomfield, and all the right people got in on the action. At the helm was Ken Friedman—a former music manager who helped turn the restaurant into an overnight hot spot. In- vestors included Jay-Z, Michael Stipe, Bono, and, most impor- tant, my idol, Mario Batali. I would sit at the low-lit amber bar in the raucous, kitsch-adorned room. I'd start a meal with the gnudi—an ethereal dish that is somehow both light and heavy at the same time. Ricotta dumplings bathing in a brown butter sauce with crispy sage. Then I'd move on to the burger— a ground trinity of brisket, short rib, and chuck, served me- dium rare, with a generous heaping of Roquefort cheese on a toasted bun. No substitutions.* The meal would end with one of April's rich-beyond-belief desserts—my favorite was the banoffee pie. I typically gravitated toward subtle sweets, but this pie was so blatantly on the other end of the spectrum, it felt like it was taunting me. A thin, buttery crust, under a layer of sliced bananas, smothered in a warm, dense blanket of caramelized condensed milk, topped by a heaping dollop of whipped cream, and dusted with shaved dark chocolate. It's intensely sweet, but the cool cream somehow cuts through all of it, creating a yin and yang that's a party in your arteries.

April's desserts weren't just meant to fill you up and send you home with sweet sweats. They were a statement. The meals at most other high-end restaurants ended with a dénouement—a small something or other upon leaving to round out the symphony of a meal. April's meals were no symphony. They were loud, messy, cacophonous harmony. They were Nirvana—the state of mind *and* the band. That dessert didn't say, "Thank you for joining us; have a great evening." It exclaimed, "Can you hear me now?"†

This era was the heyday of zero carbs, gluten substitutions, fat-free everything, dressing-on-the-side culture. People saw restaurants more as a place to get exactly what they wanted than a place to experience someone's artistic expression on a plate. The Spotted Pig defiantly stood against the traditional restaurant ethos. The customer wasn't always right. In fact,

---

*Except for neighborhood regular Lou Reed, who was allowed to get a slice of red onion on his. In the words of Mel Brooks, "It's good to be the king."

†There was actually another dish that took this sentiment a bit too literally. An occasional appetizer was the pig ear salad, which was simply a whole pig ear, deep-fried, put in the middle of the plate, and surrounded by dressed greens. It was crunchy, cartilaginous, vinegary, jarring. We can hear you now.

the customer had better shut the fuck up and enjoy the show. If you ate at the Spotted Pig, that said something about you. You were a culinary daredevil, someone who chewed first and asked questions later. The Pig was a celebrity magnet in the traditional sense, but just saying you ate there made you a celebrity.

Aside from celebs and foodies, the Pig was always full of chefs from other restaurants. This was where they came to eat truly interesting food, food they didn't have the balls to serve at their own restaurants. In the comedy world, a handful of stand-ups are considered "comics' comics." They don't have mass appeal, they're never going to have their own TV show, but they push the envelope in such interesting ways that when they're onstage, though the crowd might be unamused, the back of the room is full of cackling comics who can't get enough. Hence the expression "playing to the back of the room." April was a chef's chef. She played to the back of the room, and it was glorious.

When I told Tim about my forthcoming cooking classes, he countered with, "Why don't you just work here? You'll learn a ton more and you won't pay a cent." I ruminated on a bite of spongy calf liver drenched in caramelized onions and vinegar and took a swig of warm mulled wine. A week later, I was in the kitchen wearing a chef's toque.

Working in a kitchen in New York in the early aughts was invigorating. The flames of Anthony Bourdain's bad-boy food memoir *Kitchen Confidential* were still blazing, celebrity chefs were elevated to rock-star status, and TV shows were making kitchens look like pressure-cooker culinary fraternities where you got ruthlessly hazed in pursuit of making great food. I was used to cutthroat environments, having come up in comedy clubs,* so I was ready to take all the abuse necessary, and was even looking forward to it.

You can imagine my surprise, and even disappointment, when I walked into the kitchen at the Spotted Pig on my first day as a summer intern and was greeted by the owner and head chef herself, April Bloomfield. She brought me in for a hug and said, "Hey, Dan the Intern! I'm April. We're excited to have you." What? No "Who the hell are you?" No "What the fuck are you doing here?" I was expecting her to peg a beet at my face and call me a little bitch. "Come here," she said, walking me over to a cauldron of simmering beef tongues. She ripped off a steaming piece with her hand, split it in two, and handed me one piece. "Here, what do you think?" It was piping hot, but she didn't flinch so neither did I. We both took bites. The tongue melted in my mouth, splashing it in briny vinegary goodness. "It's unbelievable!" "Glad you like it. Welcome to the Spotted Pig." She patted me on the shoulder and walked off. At the Spotted Pig, they didn't break bread, they broke beef tongue.

The kitchen at the Spotted Pig was cartoonishly small. In a space of about two hundred square feet, some of the most memorable Michelin-starred dishes ever served in New York were made. My first task was chopping chives. Apparently, chive chiffonade is a rite of passage to working in a kitchen. At the Pig, the chive confetti garnishes the deviled eggs, almost as an afterthought. But making these green microcylinders is a perfect first task to learn the three main tenets of the kitchen:

---

*And premed at Johns Hopkins.

Be precise; be clean; keep your knife sharp. A couple of hours into my chive chopping, which apparently I kept messing up, Josh Schwartz, the sous-chef, came over to me. "These are bruised. No worries. You'll get better. Let me show you around." He threw out my chives and walked me around the restaurant.

The space was split into four floors.

Basement: Most of the grunt work took place here. Peas got shelled; fish got gutted; hulking sides of pig, beef, and lamb were broken down; and the world-famous gnudi were rolled out. Only a privileged few could make the gnudi, I learned. The recipe was kept secret even from fellow employees. The staff downstairs consisted of three Mexicans and two Ecuadorans, who were all maximum five foot three. There must've been a height requirement, as the ceiling went to only about five feet five inches.*

Ground Floor: This was where the main bar, dining room, and kitchen were—all in about one thousand square feet. The bar was small and cramped; the dining room had weird angles, and tiny stools were stuffed into corners that were never intended to be sat in. The ceilings were low, the lights were dim, and the walls were *filled* with British kitsch—a gnome here, a miniature Big Ben there, mismatched wallpaper. It was as if the interior designer shopped exclusively at a hoarder's home in Liverpool. But it worked so well. You felt like you were dining in a warm British dollhouse that just happened to

---

*Spanish class should be mandatory in culinary school. Being a non-Latino who speaks Spanish gave me an incredible amount of street cred, and I ended up learning as much from this crew as I did from the classically trained chefs. More important, being called "culo" has nothing to do with being cool.

be filled with figurines like Rihanna, Chris Martin, and Anna Wintour.

The kitchen was tucked in the back. In a space where a normal kitchen would house one or two prep stations, the Pig crushed in seven: Hots, Colds, Grill, Sauté, Veg, Expo (also known as the Pass), and Dishpit.* At most times, the cramped space, with seven cooks resolutely prepping, was *very* hot. We toweled off our sweaty brows, inhaled water from plastic storage containers, and every few minutes someone took a deep breath to recenter in the swelter. During service, however, it was a Dante's inferno, buzzing with frantic energy that did not let up for four hours. The sounds were dizzying—shoestring potatoes frying in oil, animal flesh† sizzling, chefs yelling "Behind! Hot!" as they rushed in back of you with scalding whatnot. I was expecting the kitchen to be hot, but the tiny space at the Pig was torturous. During a particularly blistering service, when I was working the fryer, my eyes started stinging. I pulled out my contacts and realized they were warping from the heat.

Second Floor: Yet another bar and dining room. Snacks were served from this bar—oysters, deviled eggs with homemade olive oil mayo, and my favorite bar snack, the chicken liver toast. Served on a thick slab of peasant bread, this was not the smooth chicken liver mousse you get at most fancy restaurants. It was a roughly chopped mess mixed with shallots, and a fifty-fifty of port and Madeira that got reduced to a syrup and bound together the minced offal. It wasn't reinventing the

---

*Read it again. It's "dish . . . pit." Not "dip . . . shit." I keep messing it up myself.
†And occasionally human.

wheel. It was finding an abandoned wheel in a barn and re-storing it to look better than it originally did.

Top Floor: This was my favorite floor. At night it was a secret dining room, accessed by a hidden stairway off the second floor. It looked more like someone's slick apartment than a restaurant, an enchanting space. Here private parties were held, and super-duper celebs would hang out. Jay-Z and Beyoncé were regulars up here.[*] This room was sexy and cool, but the daytime recipe testing here made it special to me. I *loved* it up there. It was bright and open, a sanctuary from the frantic kitchen down-stairs. Once I was up there alone with April, jazz playing as we prepped that day's farmers market haul: freshly picked chante-relle mushrooms that smelled of ripe apricots. Scapes, the long thin green shoots that taste like vegetal garlic. Dill flowers like tiny yellow flavor fireworks. One day I organized heirloom to-matoes into a rainbow of color ranging from bright red to purple to green. I remember looking at the tray, at April, at the cobble-stone charm of the West Village out the window, and thinking, "I have arrived." April took a liking to me, and we had a great relationship, mostly, I imagine, because the stakes were low. She knew I wasn't going to become a chef, and I knew I never needed her for more than instruction. My respect for her was familial. I loved her food, I loved her restaurant, I loved her.[†]

One thing people often say when they meet a professional comedian is how different they are onstage from off. That's because a good comedian's act doesn't mirror their outward

---

[*] Jay-Z actually owned the building. His name was on the lease downstairs. In a tiny frame in an inconspicuous corner was the city deed with the name "Shawn Carter" in a tiny font. Probably the most understated thing with Jay-Z's name on it.

[†] Also, I'm straight and she's gay, so none of that mishegas.

personality. It is a door into what lies beneath. It is an expression of who we *really* are when society's mask is off. That's how I understand April's connection to her food. If you met her on the street, you would say she's shy, tender, sweet, and motherly in her affection. Not the type of person you would associate with dishes like sliced beef tongue with salsa verde, croutons, and egg, or grilled striped bass with cockles and chorizo broth, or pork faggots*—a sausage of sorts filled with ground pork liver, pork cheeks, and farro, an ancient grain from the Mediterranean that sustained the Roman legions.

April taught me how to make stocks (throw in a pig's foot to add sticky, lip-smacking goodness), how to macerate strawberries (don't let the balsamic overpower the vodka and vice versa), how to make pesto (put in enough cheese to give it texture, but not so much that it tastes cheesy; it should taste like basil)—all without the aid of recipes or measuring cups. She taught me what I came to the Pig to learn: how to cook food by relying solely on my senses. This was the greatest lesson anyone could teach me. My kitchen was no longer a chemistry lab where ingredients were weighed, measured, and cooked at exact temperatures with timers and probes. It became a dance floor where I could cook anything I wanted, relying on instincts—sounds, tastes, smells, balance. I wasn't cooking with my brain; I was cooking with my whole body. My food tasted better, and my creativity was unbound. I felt free.

I loved my Spotted Pig family. And they loved me back. It was one thing to be a spectator of the New York food scene; it was another to be in the trenches of it. I loved the status my

---

*That's how it was listed on the menu. Please don't cancel me.

work gave me, the access to all the best restaurants in the country. When I would call and say I was a cook at the Spotted Pig, I was treated to tables reserved for regulars, service beyond what I thought was possible, and free dishes and drinks wherever I went. When I ate at the Pig with friends, we were treated like royalty, yet all the servers, managers, and cooks still called me "Dan the Intern," a title I wore with immense pride. My heroes were now my friends.

I often ran into Mario Batali at the bar, and even he called me Dan the Intern. It was cool knowing him, and yet at the Pig he was a lizard of a drunk. Once, I sat next to him and was telling him how much I loved working in the kitchen. Eyes part shut, stinking of grappa, he was half listening, but mostly checking out the women. One woman who was a fan came over and asked him for a picture. He obliged, then stuck his face between her breasts and motorboated her. She laughed it off but was clearly stunned by the move. He looked at me and said, "They love it," then took a swig.

It was highly unpleasant seeing Mario in the wild. His TV persona was professional, welcoming, fun. And here he was, his eyes glazed, his sausage fingers touching anyone tasty who walked by him at the bar. But truth be told, although his behavior tarnished my image of him, it wasn't enough for me to hate him. He was the person who taught me what good food was, and so what if he was a bad boy, that's what this crazy chef culture was all about, right?

When the #MeToo movement began its defiant march through misogyny in our culture, Mario Batali was the first person in the food world to be taken down. When I read the allegations, I was disgusted, but not totally surprised. He allegedly drugged and raped a woman in the private dining room of the Spotted Pig. My sanctuary. My favorite part of the restaurant was now being referred to as "the Rape Room." Friends were asking me, "Dude, did you know there was a Rape Room at the Spotted Pig when you worked there?" It wasn't the Rape Room to me; it was the Heirloom Tomato Rainbow Room. In one fell swoop, my favorite place in my favorite restaurant had been befouled, and one of my food gods was disgraced.

Months later, Ken Friedman, the Pig's co-owner, was taken down too. I grimaced reading the vile texts he wrote to one of my server friends asking for "sexy pics," repulsively persistent against a machine-gun barrage of what were clear noes from her. He forced kisses on others. Staff friends were now on *60 Minutes* talking about how awful it was to be at the Spotted Pig. I felt gutted.

April was next. She had been complicit in a lot of the awful behavior at the restaurant and hadn't done enough to stop it. Her defense was that Ken was emotionally abusive to her as well. She said he would threaten to revoke her green card, tell her she'd be nothing without him, and fly off the handle. She tried desperately to maintain her success with hard work and perfectionism, and sometimes that meant ignoring complaints from the staff, accusations that could rock what was already a very janky Michelin-starred boat. She and Ken split up as business partners in an effort to save the Pig, but it was too little, too late. Staff started to leave, morale was low, and the Spotted Pig eventually closed in 2020.[*]

---

[*]As of the writing of this chapter, Mario Batali was dropped as host of ABC's *The Chew* (which has since been canceled), sold all of his shares of his restaurant empire, and settled for $600,000 with his accusers. This former fixture of New York City now lives a hermit's

My pain comes nowhere close to the agony of the actual victims of this rot. But that doesn't mean I don't feel betrayed. Food was my religion, and my gods were apparently rapists, perverts, and apologists. Thinking back on my days as Dan the Intern, I feel a sense of stain. All my opinions on food and cooking come from this house of ill repute. I thought I was at the right place at the right time—the front lines of a food revolution that I somehow talked myself into. But the opposite was true. I was in the wrong place at the wrong time. I used to proudly proclaim my association with the Spotted Pig. Now I mostly say I worked at a Michelin-starred restaurant. I interned for free, but I paid a price. My most cherished skill set, being able to blissfully whip up delicious food relying solely on my instincts, is shackled to a colossal shame. I have no choice but to think about it every time I'm in the kitchen.

---

life in his home on Lake Michigan. When he does venture out, furtive snaps impale him on social media. Ken Friedman settled for $240,000 with his accusers, tried to open an antiques shop on Long Island to sell trinkets, and failed. April has left all seven of the amazing restaurants she helped create in New York and L.A., and is the "culinary adviser" deep behind the gates at the Vanderbilt hotel—a mansion in Newport, Rhode Island.

4

MEDITATIONS ON FALAFEL PHIL

ON MY PODCAST, *GREEN EGGS AND DAN,* THE FIRST QUESTION I ASK all my guests is "What is your earliest food memory?" The answers always provide a fun window into their lives. Chef Jacques Pépin can still conjure the deliciously warm glass of milk fresh from a cow's udder in the French countryside where his mother sheltered him while his father was fighting with the French Resistance during World War II.

My friend comedian Michelle Buteau remembers sitting on the kitchen counter next to a large enameled cast-iron pot over a steady heat. The occasional oil splatter burned her arm, but the pain was easily forgotten after her first bite of Mom's perfectly cooked fried chicken.

Phil Rosenthal, the creator of *Everybody Loves Raymond* and host of my favorite food show, *Somebody Feed Phil,* doesn't forget the off-putting chewy gray steak his mother cooked. He'd pretend to eat it, store it in his cheeks, then run to the bathroom and spit it out.

Padma Lakshmi reminisced about daring to climb a table to reach a perilously high counter in her grandmother's home in Madras, India, for the perfect jar of pickles. Her rogue mission ended on a floor blanketed in broken glass, oil, and chilies. After a slight castigation, she was given a bite of the briny goodness she had risked her six-year-old life for. It was worth all the effort.

Every guest's memory is either 100 percent positive or 100 percent negative.* My first food memory lives in a nostalgic purgatory. It started as a tale of love, but over time veered to the negative, and is now somewhere in between.

When I was five, my parents took my brothers and me to Israel. It was my first time out of the country, and my first time experiencing the explosive Middle Eastern flavors of the Levant. My memory of the trip itself is foggy. When doing research for this chapter I asked my mother to send me pictures from that time, and in one I'm holding an M16 rifle. Feels like something a kid would remember, yet I have no recollection of it. What I *do* remember, though, is my first falafel sandwich.

The environs remain vague. It was outside, nighttime; there was a train track nearby; I remember a bright lightbulb in one of those metal cones with a clip—the same setup I used as a heat lamp for my iguana.† And I remember steam. So I'm as-

---

*Weirdly enough, all my guests who have negative memories are Jews, but that's another story.
†Yeah. I had a pet iguana. His name was Iggy. I'd have long conversations with him because I had no friends. And my parents wonder why I became a comedian.

suming we were at an outdoor vendor. What needs no sleuthing is the magic of this sandwich. I remember the colors—tan from the fresh warm pita, ivory from the smattering of tahini, bright orange from the amba,* and then three or four dark crimson falafel balls on the surface of the sandwich sticking out of the sauciness like sea mines. I remember my first bite. My teeth felt like a drill going through the crust of the earth and experiencing all the different striations on the way to the treasure at the center. The dough, my god, the dough. It had a warm steamy yeastiness that tasted ancient and comforting. Shattering the plush warm calm was the rush of nutty tanginess from the tahini, the fermented fruitiness of the amba, competing with the soothing coolness of the chopped cucumbers, tomatoes, and herbs. Then came the falafel balls. A thick, crunchy exoskeleton reluctantly collapsing under my teeth's pressure, letting them sink at last into the sublime spongy earthiness of the chickpea flour. My mouth didn't know what to make of this flavor combination. My mom tells me I just kept saying, "What is this?" Little did I know that the answer, "falafel," would one day be a defining ingredient of my identity.

The Olympics for every young comedian is the Montreal comedy festival. In 2009, at age thirty-one, I was finally accepted into the New Faces show—every young comic's gateway to Hollywood. Though I had zero national recognition, I was a seasoned stand-up by this time, having performed cease-

---

*Amba is one of the best condiments you've never had. Fermented mango. Trust me, it tastes better than it sounds. Try it on grilled meats, in a salad—I'll even have it on ice cream. Keep it on hand but take it off the counter if Padma is coming over—this was the pickle she was reaching for.

lessly over the past decade in forty-nine states.* That much stage time was great, and it turned me into a strong comic. But the real silver lining was being able to experience the food scene in every hardscrabble town in our nation. The best BBQ in North Carolina, the best lobster roll in Maine, Hot Browns in Kentucky, fried alligator in Louisiana—I was a regular Guy Fieri, except I was visiting more than diners, drive-ins, or dives. The five hundred dollars I made at a show in Northern California was promptly spent a few hours later on a solo dinner at the French Laundry in Napa Valley. Stand-up became a vehicle to take my food obsession on the road.

While at the Montreal comedy festival, I made sure to fill my days with culinary adventures in what has become my favorite food town in North America. Montreal's cuisine is a perfect fusion of the finesse of French cookery with the excesses of hearty Canadian lumberjack fare. It's cultural appropriation at its best.

The festival was exhilarating, and the New Faces comics were top-notch: Kumail Nanjiani, Pete Holmes, Rory Scovel, Moshe Kasher—amazing talents from New York and L.A. whom I had never met because of my road work. The show went so well that I secured a spot on *The Tonight Show* before the festival was over. At moments in my twenties, when I was traveling the country from college to college, I downplayed my success and thought I should instead be staying in New York and L.A. to get discovered. But now being onstage with serious comics, and getting a spot amid late-night royalty, made me feel like my career was finally on track.

---

*Damn you, Hawaii!

There's a great piece of career advice I was given early on: "Don't move to L.A. until L.A. asks you to move there." Well, L.A. seemed to be finally making her request. The *Tonight Show* set went great, and I was getting calls from all the network development execs for meetings. In short order I packed up and moved to L.A.

My meetings were stellar. Networks then had just started to look for Middle Eastern voices to put on TV and in movies. I was meeting in penthouse boardrooms with huge marble tables and FIJI Water as far as the eye could see. Heads of networks were asking for my opinion of the state of Middle Eastern comedy. I always gave them the same response—"I don't consider myself to be a Middle Eastern comic. I consider myself to be a comic who happens to be Middle Eastern." They would perk up, mostly, I imagine, because though they were under pressure to deliver more diversity, they didn't want to alienate the masses. And I was on the same exact page, but for different reasons.

This was about a decade after 9/11, and there was weirdness about where Middle Eastern people fit in the new cultural landscape. While I embraced my heritage, before 9/11 I definitely used it as a comedy crutch. I used to do this stupid bit called Instant Terrorist about the best way to cut the line at the airport. Then I'd pull a belt and a towel out of a bag, put the towel on my head, wrap the belt around it, and start screaming "Allahu Akbar."* After 9/11, I tried this bit and had a beer bottle thrown at me, and the bouncers had to wrestle an angry

---

*I know. My heritage doesn't quite jibe with this portrayal. I'm Jewish, not Muslim. Also, I'm Iranian, not Arab. But my eyebrows are very much in line with the joke, and that's all that matters to an audience. Like I said—very stupid bit.

firefighter off me. So for the next few years I hid my heritage from the crowd, and suddenly I was taking triple connecting flights to colleges in the nation's heartland. I saw my stand-up jaunts around Middle America as perfect opportunities to be an ambassador for my maligned people, not by knocking audiences over the head with my Persian-ness, but by flanking them with laughter. My ethnicity became an afterthought, which let people second-guess their prejudices. It's something I call Anchovy Diplomacy. Everyone thinks they hate anchovies, but if they're diluted in a sauce, they create a taste explosion that wins over even their biggest slanderers.

While Middle Eastern comics started to lean into their ethnicity with shows like the Axis of Evil Comedy Tour and the Camels of Comedy, I prided myself on *not* participating in this stuff. Though I missed a lot of paying gigs, my Anchovy Diplomacy seemed to be paying off. Now I was being accepted into the Hollywood halls of greatness, and we were striding forward together.

I was driving from a meeting at FOX to a meeting with NBC when I received a call from my manager at the time. He was a human lizard in bedazzled leather coats, cowboy boots, and True Religion jeans. But he had gotten a bunch of people on *Saturday Night Live* a decade earlier, and that was enough to keep me working with him. His cadence was that of someone who had just snorted an Ambien and swigged a pint of molasses.

"Hey, bud, ready for some good news?"[*]

"Yeah! What's up?"

---

[*] Imagine this taking him fifteen seconds to say.

"I got you your first audition."

An exec at FOX had just said that I could be the Middle Eastern Seinfeld, and now I was getting my first audition. Best. Day. Ever.

"Amazing! What is it for?"

"It's for a new show on the Disney Channel."

Pause.

"The Disney Channel? I don't want to do a show on the Disney Channel."

"Danny boy, do you have any idea how many people watch the Disney Channel?"

"Yeah, but I'm meeting with real networks, man."

"Okay, well, here's why you should at least go on the audition. The casting director is a friend. She casts all the best shows on TV. Just go in, read for it, and make the relationship. You won't do the show."

That sounded reasonable. I needed to start building contacts.

"Okay, send it to me."

The audition was for a show called *Kickin' It*. A couple of kids hang out in a karate dojo. Cute. What wasn't cute was my role, a character named, I kid you not, Falafel Phil.

I called my manager back.

"I'm not fucking doing an audition for a racist Middle Eastern character named Falafel Phil."

"You're not going to do it, buddy. Relax. You're just going to meet the casting director."

That night, as I was committing the audition to memory, I was fuming. Here's the copy:

THE KIDS ARE SITTING AT A TABLE IN FALAFEL PHIL'S
RESTAURANT TALKING ABOUT STARTING A BOY BAND WHEN PHIL
OVERHEARS.

PHIL *[broken English]*: You want to start a boy band? I was a part
of a boy band in my home country of Hachmachistan! Who
could forget our hit song, "Baby's Got Da Noush."
PHIL SINGS "BABY'S GOT DA NOUSH."
[Please ask actor to make up a song named "Baby's Got Da Noush."]

I had gone from crafting a perfect late-night TV set to writing "Baby's Got Da Noush" in less than a month.

I met the casting director, who was lovely, and I did my audition. On my drive home my manager called.

"Great news, buddy. You got the part."

"What? I don't want the part!"

"You've been in L.A. for a week, I get you a part, and you
don't want it?"

"That's exactly right. We spoke about this."

"Look. It's one episode. It would be very disrespectful to the
casting director if you didn't do it."

I was livid. How could I face my cool new Montreal comedian friends? When they'd ask, "How did things go after the
festival?" I'd have to answer, "Oh, awesome. I landed the role
of Falafel Phil. He's from Hachmachistan." And my family!
Proud people who'd escaped Iran to give their kids a better
life, not to have their kids shit on their culture.

At the next day's table read, I did my version of "Baby's Got
Da Noush" in front of the actors, their parents, the writers,

and the network. I stole the melody from one of my favorite Arab singers, Oum Kalthoum,* and used these words:

Yalla habibi, baby's got da Noush,
You know it baby, yeah we got da Noush

Etcetera . . .

When I started singing, the room of white people went *nuts*. To me it was gross. Only as a last resort do I chalk things up to racism, but there was definitely some token Orientalism going on. At the wardrobe department they fitted me with bland khakis, a black apron, and a yellow polo shirt with FALAFEL PHIL embroidered on the chest. The wardrobe person did final touches and said, "Wow, you actually look like one of those gross falafel guys." I was angry, but said nothing because it was my first day of acting and I didn't want to ruffle feathers . . . for a role I didn't want in the first place. I was confused as the experience slowly chiseled away at my pride.

A huge studio audience teemed with kids, and a warm-up DJ played loud music and tossed candy to supercharge them between shoots. When it was time for my scene, I jumped on-stage, amped up by the sugary prediabetic juveniles before me. If my performance at the table read was a six, this was a twelve. The kids went crazy. And I'm not going to lie, I enjoyed it. It was my first TV show, with cameras, lights, a live audience—it was electric. I was happy for the experience—and thrilled I would never have to do it again.

---

*Feel free to sue Disney for the rights, Oum!

At home that night, I got a call from my manager.

"Hey, buddy, I heard you did great."

"Yeah, it was . . . whatever."

"Glad you loved it, because guess what? They want to make you a part of the show. They're going to build out a whole restaurant just for you. You made it. You're on a TV show."

"No, I told you, I'm not doing this role."

"What do you mean? You were just offered a TV show. How are you not going to do it?"

"We talked about this. You said I didn't have to do this hacky shit."

"It would be *extremely* disrespectful to the producers if you didn't do the show. They're building a restaurant for you, Dan."

I was torn. I was tired of doing the road and scrambling to colleges for money. Here was an opportunity to finally get out of that world, *but* at the expense of my self-respect. As much as my manager filled me with bad advice, the choice was always mine. I tried to look at the bright side. I'd get good experience on a set, and I would be on a kids' show, so I would stay under the radar. Ha!

Falafel Phil became the breakout star of the show and adoring fans were mobbing me on the streets. The more people loved my character, the more Disney wrote me in. I was stuck. And, sure, some of you readers are thinking, "What's wrong with this guy? He's acting on a TV show and complaining about it? He's living the dream!" Let me give you some elements of this dream that made me so conflicted.

Falafel Phil was from the fictitious country of Hachmachistan. I know you know this already, but what the fuck?

His first job in America was a speed bump.

Falafel Phil's chef was his pet goat, Tootsie.

Falafel Phil had a picture of him and Tootsie in a heart on his mantel, suggesting a will-they-won't-they with the goat.

He has a niece, Mika, played by a very attractive actress. However, Phil thinks she's ugly because in Hachmachistan, what's beautiful is ugly and what's ugly is beautiful.

Instead of saying, "You're not pulling the wool over my eyes," Phil says, "You're not pulling the yak fur over my seeing balls."

Falafel Phil's sister, Phyllis (played by me in drag), boasts about shaving her mustache to come see him.

The list goes on. While my role ingratiated me with children, I kept Falafel Phil secret from my fellow comedians, family, friends, and women I dated. Sometimes it didn't work. Because kids don't get the concept of boundaries, they would just run up to me at inopportune times. I remember being on dates, trying to be suave, when suddenly a group of eager five-year-olds would run to the table and start singing "Baby's Got Da Noush."*

As I became more and more enmeshed in Falafel Phil, other career opportunities fell through. Meanwhile, my Montreal friends were skyrocketing to fame. Kumail Nanjiani was starring on HBO's *Silicon Valley,* Pete Holmes was hosting his own talk show on TBS, Moshe Kasher had just gotten a deal at

---

*Although I'll admit, one of the greatest moments of my life happened that way. I was seated in the dentist's waiting room, next to a little girl, when the door opened, and in walked Matthew McConaughey, who sat next to us. As I shook with nerves, the little girl looked up and said, "Excuse me, sir, are you an actor?" McConaughey, in his deep Texas drawl, said, "Why, yes, little girl, I am." "Not you," she said and pointed to me, asking the most glorious question I've ever been asked: "Are you Falafel Phil?" You bet your ass I am.

Comedy Central. My fame was rising too, but with the wrong audience and for the wrong reasons. When a kid learned I was Falafel Phil, and asked if all people from the Middle East had pet goats as girlfriends, I was aghast to see I was infecting a new generation with searing, vile stereotypes.

Another low was when Falafel Phil's sister, Phyllis, comes to town. I played Phyllis, complete with frumpy dress and painted unibrow. Phyllis and Phil get in a fight and yell a bunch of Arab-sounding gibberish at each other. Years later, this clip went viral on Twitter with the caption "Can you believe Disney allowed this racist bullshit?" They tagged me on it to shame me, but I agreed with them. However, I didn't agree with a subgroup on Twitter that found out I was an Iranian Jew and accused me of being a Mossad spy trying to foment anti-Arab hate in the world. I can assure you that is not the case.*

Kickin' It lasted four seasons and was one of Disney's most successful shows ever.† When I finally finished my tenure as Falafel Phil, I was desperate to re-create myself and move on to the next gig. Falafel Phil could not be my legacy. So I went on a tear, auditioning for anything, any roles—except those with accents. I was being called in for parts that I was clearly not right for. At one audition I was supposed to play the head of the CIA. What? I could maybe play the bumbling security

---

*Or, I *am* a spy, and this insane long game of a scheme had as one of its bullet points: "Write a chapter about Falafel Phil in a book eight years after the role is over." Those wily Zionists.

†Anytime I post anything on my Instagram, half the comments are from kids writing "Falafel Phil!" When I wrote a post protesting anti-Semitic hate crimes in the United States the first person who responded asked, "Are you Falafel Phil?" I replied, "Seems like a weird time to ask, but yes. I'm Falafel Phil." If you don't believe me, I've pinned the comment. Search for @standupdan and look for the blue square.

guard searching Craigslist for a used mattress, ignoring the CCTV while terrorists breach the Pentagon doors. But the head of the CIA? In the waiting room with me was a bunch of tall Jon Hamms, six-foot-plus, chiseled jawlines, perfect noses. When I finally made it into the audition room, the casting director, the director, and the network executive were all there. This was weirdly high-level for a first read. They turned on the camera and I did my best CIA chief.

"Mr. President. This is not a drill. I need you to be decisive. And if you won't be"—pause—"I will."

The network executive chimed in.

"That was great, Dan, thanks so much for coming in."

"Thank you. Do you want me to try it a different way?"

"No, that was great." They didn't want me. Shocker.

"Oh, Dan, before you go. My daughter's birthday is this weekend, and she's a big fan of your Disney character."

She pulled out her phone.

"Would you mind making a quick video for her? Her name is Melody."

I died a little inside. "Yeah, no problem." She pointed her iPhone at me. "Again, Melody, and she's turning nine."

"Yup, got it." I died a little more. "Hey, Melody, it's Dan Ahdoot, just wanted to wish you a *very* happy ninth birthday, have a great time with your friends and—"

The executive stopped shooting. "I'm sorry, Dan, would you mind doing it as the character? Falafel Frank?" Snickers from the others in the room.

"Phil. It's Falafel Phil. Sure, I can do that." I was dead. I did what she asked, in that awful voice, in front of the kingmakers who saw me as the joke I had become.

All my hard work, all my toiling and traveling, all my attempts to maintain my integrity and not use my ethnicity for a crutch—all for naught. If only I had been as decisive as the fake CIA director I stupidly thought I had a chance of playing. If only I had told my manager, "No. I will not play this hacky, stereotypical garbage character." But I felt I had no choice—especially at the time. There was no room for any people of color in shows. There were a couple of industry darlings—Aziz Ansari and Kumail Nanjiani—and the rest of us had to choose between terrorists and Falafel Phil. I realized Phil made it impossible for me to get another acting role. I debated quitting the business and going back to medical school, or going into cooking, which was always a passion of mine. I was ready to walk.

I confided in one of the writers of *Kickin' It* I had befriended, David Bickel. He told me that if the world saw me only as Falafel Phil, it was my job to show them something else. "Write yourself the role you want." "I don't know how to write TV." "So learn." And that's what I did. I took classes, went to lectures, did everything I could do to learn a craft that might get me out of the mess I'd gotten myself into. I asked my manager to set me up with producers, but he wouldn't. He didn't think I had enough experience as a writer, and whenever I tried to convince him to take a chance on me, he would come back with some generic manager bullshit.

"Please, man, just get me in the room."

"Dan, who is on your Mount Rushmore of comedians?"

Sigh.

"You ask me this question every year. Can you please just set me up with a producer?"

"Mount Rushmore. Who's on it."

"Louis C.K., Chris Rock, Dave Attell, Patton Oswalt."

"You need to look at their careers and try to emulate them. Listen, I gotta go, I have another call."

That last indignity sent me to my storage, where I pored over all the business cards I had collected at the Montreal comedy festival five years earlier and emailed all of the executives myself. One of them got back to me: a producer named Marcus Wiley. He asked me to come in with any show ideas I might have.

I worked furiously to come up with some real gems for the meeting. I saw this as my final chance to eke something out of the ashes of my career. The waiting room was dotted with posters of Marcus's hit shows. The assistant, Jacqui,* brought me FIJI Water.† I could hear Marcus finishing up an important call—talking about actor fees that were in the hundreds of thousands of dollars. His conversation was still going on when Jacqui walked me in.

I sat on a couch across from him; he smiled and raised a *one more minute* finger. "Okay, sounds good. We'll start production on the fifteenth. Yeah. You know I love you. Okay. Take care." He hung up and put out his hand. "Hi, Dan, Marcus Wiley."

Marcus was strikingly handsome, half Black, half Asian, charming and warm. He walked over to the Nespresso machine and made us both coffees. After some small talk, I

---

*Sweet spelling.

†FIJI Water is the official water of serious Hollywood meetings. It's like they want you to know that they went out of their way to cause the highest carbon footprint to quench your thirst.

launched into my ideas. Each one was meticulously thought out and I delivered them with passion, optimism, everything I had. When I finished up the third idea, he took a final sip of his espresso, put it down, and gave me a devastating, limp "That was good; those were good." "You don't like them," I said. "It's not that I don't like them, I just don't really see why these ideas are important to you."

Why they're important to me? They're the last thing between my dream of being a comedian and getting a day job! There was an awkward pause. I did what I always do: I steered the conversation to food. "Bummer. I guess I'll cancel the reservation I made at Spago for us to celebrate." He perked up. "Spago is awesome." He started to tell me about his favorite restaurants in L.A. I told him mine, and the momentum was back. Then the conversation switched to best food cities in America. I told him I obviously thought New York was number one,[*] but if we expanded the conversation to North America, Montreal was the clear winner. I was grasping at straws, just trying to extend my time in his office. It might be the last time I would be in a producer's office. As we started comparing Montreal places—Joe Beef, Au Pied de Cochon, Le Vin Papillon—he stopped and stared at me as if for the first time.

"Wait a second. Did you do New Faces at Montreal?"

"Yeah! That's where I got your card."

"You had that bit about Jewish sign language, right?"

"Yeah, that was me."

He adjusted in his seat. "Dan, I thought you had the best set of that class."

---

[*] I've since changed my tune. GO, L.A., GO!

"Wow, thanks."

"This is going to sound offensive, and I don't mean it to be, but how did you not explode after that? You're hilarious. What happened?"

My lips started to tremble.

"Falafel Phil happened."

"What?"

"Falafel Phil fucking happened!"

"What are you talking about?"

I launched into my saga. "Wait," said Marcus, "is this a bit?" "NO, DUDE." At first he didn't believe me. I handed him my laptop and asked him to google Falafel Phil, and he watched one of the insane videos of my character. I took him through every part of the journey. Feeling trapped, taken advantage of, bullied, trying to keep my professional life a secret, watching enviously as everyone around me went on to great things while I was in a tryst with a fucking goat, completely derailed from where I wanted to be. Marcus's howling even brought Jacqui in to hear my tirade. She wanted in on the joke of my life.

After what seemed like an hour of my venting, with the two of them at the edge of their seat, Marcus stood up, ambled to his bar, and poured three Scotches. "Dan," he said. "This is your show."

Over the next month I moved into Marcus's office, and he helped me craft a pitch for a show called *Dan Derailed*. Mapping out all the characters, all the plot points, season arcs, all the pitfalls, all the drama, all the comedy. We took the idea to FOX, and met with the executives in a huge boardroom, around a marble table, overlooking all of L.A., FIJI Water abounding*—the same room I was meeting in after the Montreal comedy festival. I sold the show for $125,000, more money than I had ever made in my life. I was stunned. I didn't even know this concept of selling shows existed, and for the next five years it became my main source of income—all thanks to Falafel Phil and Marcus Wiley. I had a new lease on my career. I'm positive that having to dig myself out of the hole of Falafel Phil forced me to do things I wouldn't normally do, and ultimately made me a stronger performer and turned me into a writer. And here we are, on Chapter 4 of a frigging book.†

What outweighs any professional gains from playing Phil is the reactions on kids' faces when they see me. When you're recognized for an adult role, what you get is usually a fist bump or a selfie. But when a five-year-old fan sees you in real life, they think you're the actual character you play, and they beam with joy. It's such a genuine love, it slaps any cynicism out of me. I had the chance one time to visit a pediatric cancer ward as Falafel Phil, which ended with me and about fifteen kids with leukemia singing "Baby's Got Da Noush" at full volume, accent and all, for everyone on the floor to hear. I put my shame out there for them in the best way I could, and they loved me for it.

It's easy to claim I was just an unwitting pawn in a racist entertainment machine. But there's a sad fact underneath all this—I will never be able to play any role as well as I played Falafel Phil. I was custom-made for him. When I heard "Ac-

---

*Carbon schmarbon!

†BTW, that humiliating audition with the casting director *did* end up being a smart move because she cast me in *Bajillion Dollar Propertie$*, one of my favorite acting gigs. Human lizard was right about connecting with her! Broken clocks.

tion!" I sank my teeth into this juicy falafel of a role with the same joy and wonder I got from eating the sandwich in Israel. Some of it was Stockholm syndrome, sure. If I focused on the racism, that sank me deep. My choice was to go numb, or give it everything I had. I gave the character a soul. His large heart animated all the goofiness and made him resonate with the young viewers. Kids didn't love Phil because they were racist. They loved him because he was a clown. A real clown, in the classical French sense. There's an expression in clowning that I love: "The clown falls so that you don't have to." I like to take it one step further—the clown *fails* so that you don't have to. And the more authentic the failure, the bigger the laugh. As good as I was at playing a broad wacky character, I drove to and from work every day thinking I was a failure, sometimes on the verge of tears, sometimes past the verge. And that colored my role in the best possible way. Feeling like a failure while you're getting showered with the innocent accolades of children is a mindfuck of a recipe for doing my best work.

Okay. Deep breath. I say all that, to say this. I relive flickers of this saga every time I see the word "falafel." So as much as I love that haunting sandwich, for now, I'll pass. Good thing I also love shawarma. And I don't think I'll be playing Shawarma Shawn anytime soon.

5

UNDERCOOKED

I KNEW I WANTED TO MARRY ISABELLE EVEN BEFORE I MET HER. "SHE'S a chef," my friend Julia, who was setting us up, said. "Really?" "Yeah, let me show you a picture." She pulled out a shot of a fiercely athletic, petite sunflower of a girl, hair pulled back, smiling big in a fitted chef's jacket and apron, wearing Converse high-tops. "What's her ring size?" I asked, jokingly. Although months later, the question wouldn't be a joke. Our first date was shortly thereafter, and I was instantly hooked. Though I was obsessed with food, I'd never dated a chef. It was exhilarating. She recipe-tested phenomenal dishes on me nightly, eagerly awaiting my feedback. She had a large network of chef friends, and free dishes, "gifts from the kitchen," followed us everywhere we ate. She'd whisk around the world in private jets, cooking for the biggest celebrities, and I was involved in putting together the menu. Her ring size was 7.5, and six months later, a ring that size was on her finger. Sure, we had some issues, but a real good hollandaise, I thought, could cover up anything.

Months later we took a trip to Spain. We had intended to go to Italy, because we planned our journeys around the best restaurant reservations we could get. This was the way we traveled. Francis Mallmann is doing a one-night pop-up in Miami? Let's go. There's a truffle festival in the south of France one week in May? On it. King salmon season in Seattle? Calling Delta. But one table kept eluding us. For the past year we had tried to get a reservation at Osteria Francescana, at the time the number two restaurant in the world.[*] We were always met with a bunch of noes. I emailed, called, tweeted, DMed, sent dick pics, nothing. However, we *did* score a reservation to Mugaritz, a Michelin three-star restaurant near San Sebastián, Spain. And though it wasn't our top choice, we were excited. The day after landing in Spain, we got the most ill-timed email: "It is with delight that we offer you a reservation for tomorrow afternoon at 1 P.M. for lunch at Osteria Francescana." We couldn't believe it. Our dream! But also, who the fuck do these people think they are? It's a tiny restaurant in a tiny town in Italy, they know we're from the United States, yet they just assume we're going to drop everything and head to bumfuck northern Italy? Well, they were right. Sorry, Mugaritz. I changed our plane tickets, and we left for Milan that night. We took one of those shitty European discount airlines—the ones

---

[*]Number two on the S.Pellegrino list, which is kind of dubious. These fuckers won't even eat at your restaurant unless you fly them out and put them up and admire their children. One of those things isn't true, and I'm not quite sure which one.

where flying from Madrid to Milan is only like twenty dollars, but then they charge you for each piece of luggage, each carry-on item, each square of toilet paper, and thirty minutes later you land ten thousand dollars poorer.

We rented a car and drove through the pastoral northern Italian countryside where prosciutto and Parmesan cheese were invented, on the way to our destination—Modena. And man, were we stoked. We replayed the episode of *Chef's Table* in which Massimo Bottura, the charismatic chef, tells the story of how he single-handedly helped rebuild the economy of Emilia-Romagna by creating a widely circulated recipe for Parmigiano risotto that required people to buy more Parmesan cheese. Touching, but when you think of it, how hard was this situation? "Help! We just had an earthquake!" "Oh no, should we send aid? Firefighters?" "Nope, just buy the most delicious cheese ever invented." "Ahh, it feels good to do good."*

We arrived in Modena a couple of hours early and had some time to kill. We ate the most luscious artisanal gelato; Isabelle charmed the shopkeepers at the local market while I sipped an espresso and smiled; we held hands walking past the sixteenth-century church, taking in the sounds of the bells and reveling in the chirps of little kids speaking the cutest Italian. It was heaven.

We also had a "when in Rome" moment (three hours north of Rome, as it happened), where we visited an actual balsamic vinegar house in the city where this mystical ambrosia was invented. These "aceitias," as they are known, are on the out-

---

*Just kidding. It was probably way worse than this. Thoughts and prayers.

skirts of the center of town, and they are totally worth the visit. They're not quite factories, more like small villas covered in ivy that have been in the same family for generations. A pea gravel driveway dotted with cypress trees drew us from the street past the humble vineyard, right up to the home. Standing outside waving at us was a charming, well-dressed, super-handsome Italian guy named Piero, who was a fourth-generation Vinegarista.* If this guy were living in L.A., he'd be an influencer with millions of followers charging forty dollars a video on Cameo. He led us into the tasteful fresco-adorned living room of his home, and began teaching me, Isabelle, and two Dutch tourists about balsamic vinegar. He came in hot.

"Bene, who here has tried balsamic vinegar?" All hands went up. "Liars! Put your hands down. You've never tried it. I'm going to change your life." Okay, aggressive, but he was right. And I tell you now, reader, chances are you haven't had the real thing either. If you bought it in a supermarket, it's not real balsamic. If you had it at a restaurant and weren't dumbfounded by the price tag, it's not real balsamic. If it didn't come out of a bottle designed by Giorgetto Giugiaro, a dude who also designed Ferraris, it's not real balsamic.†

Piero brought out a three-generations-old earthen jar with a linen doily on top of it. He delicately removed the doily,

---

*This is not a real word, but you get it.
†These rules are really interesting. There have been yearlong court cases dedicated to what qualifies as balsamic vinegar. Largely, the good people of Modena have lost these cases, which is why you can get balsamic vinegar in an Albuquerque gas station. But to be designated actual balsamic vinegar, the grapes have to be Trebbiano harvested in Modena, they have to be aged in wooden barrels no less than twelve years, and they have to be packaged in a slick bottle fashioned by Giorgetto Giugiaro. So yeah. Calling the stuff we pick up at the supermarket balsamic vinegar is like calling Piero sort of good-looking. *He's a god among men!*

dipped a tiny spoon inside, and asked us to line up as if we were receiving Communion. One by one, we approached, and he slowly poured the spoonful into our mouths. Instantly, this liquid gold transformed us into believers. It was truly a religious experience—our sweet and sour taste buds were awakened, not with a bullhorn, but with a concerto written by a master played delicately on a Stradivarius.

Real balsamic vinegar couldn't be more different from the commercial stuff we buy. It is a tart, sweet syrup that is just concentrated fermented grape, yet it miraculously turns into an umami bomb that could make shoe leather taste divine. Also, it's crazy expensive. Maybe it was handsome Piero, maybe the setting, maybe the actual liquid, but if you told me I was going to spend five hundred dollars on vinegar, I'd say you were insane—or Piero, who literally said, "That will be five hundred dollars." As the dial-up modem from his card reader contacted American Express, he shared a philosophical moment with me in his dreamy accent: "There is something so funny about spending this much money on rotten grape juice, no? The only difference is, we rot it in the right way, and it becomes magic." I don't want to say that I got hard listening to him waxing poetic about vinegar, so I'm just going to move on.

Vinegar in tow, we were on our way to the number two restaurant in the world. We parked and started meandering through the charming, quiet cobblestone Italian streets until we saw a small gathering in the distance at what seemed to be our restaurant. "Is that a TV crew?" As we got closer, we realized it was. "Ugh, paparazzi," I joked. "They found out Falafel

Phil was in town." We figured there must be a legit celebrity there, but as we got closer, someone with a microphone came running toward us. "Are you eating at Francescana?" "Yes?" "Have you heard the news?" "No?" *Fuck me,* I thought. *The chef has killed himself.* A selfish concern, I'll admit. Someone was so tortured in his head that he ended his life, and all I could think about was "What about my pasta?"

But Massimo Bottura was not dead. In fact, he was probably the most alive he'd ever been, because an hour before, his temple to northern Italian cooking had just been crowned the world's best restaurant. We were going to be the first people to enjoy this excellence. Isabelle and I couldn't believe our luck. We had just won the foodie lottery. Bulging L5-S1 disc be damned, I picked her up, twirled her around, and we kissed to the clicks of photojournalists' cameras. Beaming, we milled about with the other lucky patrons, making small talk: "How amazing is this?" "Where are you guys from?" "Did you also just spend your life savings on vinegar?"

Suddenly the doors opened and we all quieted down. An Italian man with a Roman nose and a perfectly fitted seal-gray suit marched out, head high, smile plastered across his face, and announced: "Welcome to Osteria Francescana, the number one restaurant . . . IN THE WORLD!" We all broke out into applause. I squeezed Isabelle's hand; we looked into each other's welled-up eyes. If this wasn't true love, what was?

Osteria Francescana is a beautiful, weird establishment. When you enter, you're surrounded by provocative avant-garde art: a huge Damien Hirst spin painting, which mimics Chef Bottura's splatter-style plating, some Murakami flowers smiling in ecstasy as you walk by, a bizarre life-size sculpture of a sleeping security guard by Maurizio Cattelan.* The setting is quirky and esoteric, and so are the chef and the food. We walked into the small dining room, which seated only twenty people. We were twenty of the luckiest people in the foodie world, and we knew it.

You can go to the best restaurants in the United States, and at least 15 percent of the guests will be dressed casually. Not at Francescana. Everyone was dressed to the noves.† Each diner looked like a celebrity, even though I recognized nobody, so let's make them up. I imagine the woman with the crocodile Hermès and the oversize sunglasses was a famous opera singer. The four handsome boys in their midtwenties, wearing tight suits, loafers with no socks, and shirts open two buttons too much, were players on the Italian national polo team. And the elegant portly man with an orange pochette blooming from his double-breasted jacket pocket was a Greek shipping magnate who had to dock his yacht nearby to get gas.‡ Isabelle and I shared looks of "Can you fucking believe we're here?" It was magical. The staff was just as excited as we were.

And so it began. Osteria Francescana offers some of the most whimsical, creative food I've ever eaten. Massimo Bottura has taken classic recipes of northern Italy and re-created them in the most imaginative way possible—a tall order coming from a food culture big on sticking religiously with tradition.

---

*I totally had to look these people up. Don't think I'm this big art snob. Just food.
†"Nove" is "nine" in Italian. Kind of cute, right?
‡Not to mention his smoking-hot pop singer companion who must've won season 8 of *Athens's Got Talent*.

A lot of people have already described the place's greatest hits: The Caesar Salad in Bloom is easily the most beautiful thing I've ever eaten anywhere—a cross section of lettuce dotted with flower petals and draped with an ethereal sauce, actually earning the emperor's name in its title. The Five Ages of Parmigiano Reggiano in Different Textures and Temperatures—a love letter to the eponymous cheese, using the ingredient at different ages for different compositions—was as good as it looks on all the Netflix documentaries. And the Oops! I Dropped the Lemon Tart was a Jackson Pollock of a dessert inspired by a time when Massimo's sous-chef dropped a lemon tart on the way out of the kitchen, and Massimo re-created its entropy on a plate. But I'm not here to talk about those things. I'm here to talk about something called Risotto Levante.

This was the fifth course out of twelve, and our neurons were dining on serotonin with the same gusto with which we were enjoying Massimo's reveries. Everything was tremendous, so we were eager for what was to come next. The risotto. It was as beautifully pretentious a presentation as you could hope for. The velvety rice comes on one of those plates that is two feet wide, with a tiny divot in the middle for three spoonfuls of ecstasy. Two ninja-like, impassive servers who could've been actual descendants of Michelangelo's models stood behind us and gingerly landed the plates in front of us at exactly the same angle, with exactly the same tai chi pace. They slowly pulled back, the plates still having a gravitational pull on them, and then slinked away into the ether, clearing the way for our main waiter to take center stage.

Domenico had a perfect bald head, manicured fingers, and

just the right amount of professionalism for a high-end server.[*] He breathed in gracefully, like he was on minute four of Headspace, and delivered my favorite line of the night: "Your next course is a Risotto Levante. It is meant to evoke the salty winds coming from the Levant, washing over the Italian Peninsula from the Adriatic to the Tyrrhenian Sea." I am *in*! I love this shit. I know it's flamboyant, but it's part of the fun for me. Like when a sommelier intones about a wine you're considering that "the winemaker Mathieu lives in a hut because he likes all of the profits to go back to the vines, which are grown on a southwest slope of shale deposits from the Mesozoic era so your grapes are literally sucking minerals out of the same ground where dinosaurs stomped. That's why he named this vintage Bronto Sauvignon Blanc." I know it's a performance, but it puts me in a happy mood. I love it in the same way that I love reading fiction. Yes, the story never happened, but if it did, that would be pretty cool. Why not believe in all the pomp for the duration of your meal? "Let's agree to call bullshit on literally everything except restaurant bullshit."[†] But I digress.

Now the risotto. Domenico went off on how the risotto is made from a special grain that Marcus Aurelius himself planted, and it's cooked in a special broth that was gently heated using only the warm breath of babies, all the hoopla I love. Then he took out a spray bottle and said, "Close your eyes and take in this infusion of orange blossom and seawater which will mimic the air from the Levant which blows through or-

---

[*]He was engaging throughout the evening except for when I said, "That salad was fucking amazing." He smiled and walked away, a subtle insinuation that such language was not tolerated. Noted.
[†]My campaign slogan for 2024.

ange groves and dances above the Mediterranean before joining the risotto grains." I closed my eyes, he sprayed the dish,
and I was suddenly sitting on a jagged Mediterranean coast, a
shepherd taking a break, letting my flock wander freely while
I took my repose. I took a deep breath of the ocean, the orange
groves below, all of it nuzzling into my nasal passages and dis-
tilled into this dish. Nothing in my life could go wrong.

I took a spoonful of this glistening treasure and put it in my
mouth. The first bite* was carried in the afterglow of my shepherd life. But by bite two, the shepherd had disappeared, and I
was back sitting at the restaurant, chewing on *severely undercooked risotto.*

My first instinct was to say nothing. "It must be me. I just
don't understand the nuances of al dente risotto," I told myself.
I took another bite. Mind you, there was only one bite left, so I
took a quarter bite to be exact. This time I felt the grains give
under the pressure of my teeth and coat my mouth with what
felt like hard sand. I looked into Isabelle's eyes. "This is . . .
interesting," she said. "Yeah, it's . . . different," I added.

Because I wasn't sure Isabelle was feeling the same thing, I
thought, *I can't ruin this dish for her.* I choked down another
quarter bite of the grainy starch, and the fantasy that kicked
off the dish had curdled. I was no longer the shepherd taking
in the Mediterranean under the orange groves. I was now the
sheep on all fours grinding bites of sooty grass. I couldn't take
it anymore.

"Hey, I don't like this," I said, in a reflexive jolt. Isabelle put
down her fork in relief. "Me neither. It's really undercooked,

*Do you bite into risotto? Slurp?

right?" "One hundred percent!" We kept our comments to a barely audible whisper. Yet Domenico, like all waiters at Michelin three-star restaurants, sensed a glitch in the matrix and seemed to appear out of nowhere, gently hovering above us. "Is everything okay?" "Yes! Oh my god, yes. Amazing. Thank you." "And signora?" "Perfetto, grazie." Pleased, he nodded, and disappeared into the background.

We had a choice to make. Do we (a) force down the remaining grit of this barely edible dish, or (b) express our displeasure though only *half a bite remained,* and ask for a replacement? Know that in nearly any other restaurant, I would not hesitate. I have a lot of friends who shudder at the thought of returning dishes. Not me. I love it. Nothing gives me more pleasure. When I'm at a table of friends and one of them doesn't like a dish, I love to be the one to take control of the return—mostly because I want to see how a server responds. At good restaurants the replacement is swift and usually without question. At okay restaurants, there will be a slight tension when they take the dish away. And at shitty restaurants, there will be a debate. And that is a debate I *live* for. Why? Because most people stay silent in these situations, and I feel like I'm speaking up for all those the world over without a voice. This is my Silence Is Violence.

But how do you return a dish at a restaurant that was just named tops in the world? They got the news only an hour before we sat down, that the food served in this fifteen-hundred-square-foot space is the world's *very best*! Better than in Tokyo, better than in New York City, better than in Paris. We had just summited Mount Everest, and we were going to complain about the view?

My initial instinct was to keep chewing the orange sand, wash it down with some wine, and move on to the next course. It would be too jarring to the staff, who had toiled all their lives for this very day, and would suddenly come crashing down from their great height. But then I started thinking of *my* toils. I had worked my ass off to make the money it took to ascend to this cuisine stratosphere. I paid for plane tickets, hotels, vinegars, not to mention three hundred dollars a person for the meal *before wine pairing*. That's a lot of dick jokes to get us to sit in this restaurant. So no. I wasn't going to spare someone's feelings so that I could have a mediocre meal. Here on Everest's peak, I was going to insist that they rearrange the clouds.

I lifted a finger to summon Domenico. "Scusi." Patrons who five courses back were our compatriots now looked over curiously as if there was a chance our passports might be fake. "What could he be complaining about?" All of the staff were laser-focused on my table, already seeing this as a huge shame, that someone at the best restaurant in the world needed something he wasn't psychically offered beforehand. Domenico walked over in slow motion, his real smile quickly turning to one that was fake.

"Sì? Is everything okay?" You could hear a pin drop. I was about to bail. Just eat the half bite of sand, Dan. Fuck that. "No, actually. I feel like the risotto is a bit . . . off." Time stopped. All I heard was my heartbeat, as a bead of sweat formed on Domenico's bald head. It was as if I'd told him his mom was a whore. "Eh. What?" "A whore. Your mother is a whore." He must have assumed there was a language barrier because there was absolutely no way someone ever returned something at this restaurant, let alone on the day it was crowned king. So he excused himself and brought over the maître d', whose English was better. She was prepped by our waiter with a whisper that made her eyes bulge as if he'd told her, "Yes. A whore. My mother." Patrons were pausing mid-chew and craning to see what it was we were returning, discussing our snafu rather than focusing on their own experience. *We were ruining everyone's meal at Osteria Francescana!* What the hell did I get us into?

"Yes? Is there a problem?" "Hi, no, not a problem per se, there's, it's just . . . My girlfriend wanted to tell you something. Babe?"

Isabelle, staring daggers at me, took over reluctantly. "Yes, I'm a chef, I never return food if it's prepared correctly, and I can feel the grains of risotto in my teeth. I think it's definitely, it's . . . Dan?" Two can play at this game.

Fuck! "Undercooked!" I said. "It's undercooked." Oh boy, that was too loud. The room let out a collective gasp. The maître d' swiftly grabbed our dishes and whisked them away as if to protect the risotto from embarrassment. We then heard the muffled Italian of all the waiters huddled behind the wall that separates the dining room from the entrance: "[unintelligible Italian] . . . risotto! . . . [unintelligible Italian] . . . Americani . . . [unintelligible Italian] . . . Santa Maria!" We sat debased at our naked table, all eyes on us.

Ten grueling minutes of our lives went by until a replacement dish was dropped at our table, making a slightly louder sound than the other plates had. Loud enough for us to get the hint. However, what was on the plate was not subtle. It was a loud and clear "go fuck yourselves." The waiter cleared his throat, as if excited to deliver a guilty verdict. "Fillet of mackerel."

Now, on the surface, this is not a "go fuck yourself" substitution. But Isabelle, like a lot of people, can't stand mackerel. It was a bold move by the chef, as if to say, "You say my technique is bad? How about flawless technique on a polarizing ingredient? What now?" I like mackerel, so I was in the clear. My poor companion, however, had one of three bad choices in front of her: (1) Eat the mackerel and hate life, (2) somehow figure out a way to pass the mackerel to me so I eat it, risking offending the already frayed sensibilities of the dining room, or (3) return the mackerel and get both of us dragged into the Modena town square to be burned at the stake to a crisp, which was fitting since we didn't like things undercooked.

She went with the first option, and at what was supposed to be the best meal of her life, she ate an ingredient she would have expected in her worst. I felt bad for her. So much so that later, when we were in couples therapy, at our worst, and I had to find a memory of when I loved her, I went straight to the fifth course of our tasting menu, when she took one for the team.

I don't really remember the rest of our meal. It's hard to bounce back from a poor experience in a once-in-a-lifetime adventure. The whole point of these pretentious endeavors is that for three hours life is perfect and nothing can go wrong. It's less of a dining event and more of an art installation that you play a part in. And that risotto took down the whole veneer, from which we never recovered.

Isabelle and I had loved telling people about amazing meals we had in faraway places. We'd watch them stare in amazement, envious that we got into that impossible sushi place in Tokyo, or the glam VIP dinner in Paris, or the outrageous repast at a celebrity chef's home in Montreal. What we left out was what happened between meals. Our romance had huge foundational issues that we kept trying to cover over with food affairs. Food was about the only thing that brought us together. I did everything I could to get to Osteria Francescana less for the experience and more because I thought it would save our engagement. And if we couldn't enjoy a meal at the best restaurant in the world, it was time to call it quits. We broke up shortly after returning home.

Years later, I look back at that awful day and think that maybe it was exactly what we needed to cut the cord in a partnership that was not going to succeed no matter how many shavings of white truffles we threw at it. Even though that meal was spoiled, over time it was the best thing that could have happened to us. It was perfectly spoiled—like true balsamic vinegar.

6

ELK CAMP

MO CALLED ME IN A FRENZY. "DUDE, YOU ARE NOT GOING TO BELIEVE it. We drew elk tags for New Mexico!"* This is classic Mo. I never asked him to put in for an elk tag. But he applied for one, threw my name into the mix, and then called me so wound up that it would be hard for me to back out.

"Oh. Okay?"

"Okay? What do you mean, okay? Dude! You know how hard it is to draw these tags?"

However rare, I had won something I never really had any

---

*This is how "tags" work. Game animals, especially the big ones, are heavily regulated so their populations stay healthy. You can't walk into the woods with a gun and just shoot any creature. You need to put in for a tag, which is in essence a lottery where the winner gets the ability to kill. ALL of the tag money goes to conservation, which is why, in an ironic twist, hunters are among the highest donors to environmental conservation in the country.

interest in winning. It would be like someone calling you to say, "Congratulations! You just won a brand-new cement truck!" Still, Mo's excitement was infectious. Also, I wasn't completely averse to the idea.*

By now I had hunted deer, ducks, geese, quail, pheasants, and mourning dove. I liked to hunt, but I loved cooking with these forbidden flavors even more. Taking traditional recipes and subbing in wild game made my palate giddy with excitement. Chicken tikka masala is cool and all, but substitute pheasant and it adds a whole new level of succulent flavor that would dazzle even the most authentic of Indian chefs.†

I had never hunted elk. Of all the animals in the deer family, elk is known for being the most delicious. It's that sweet spot of slight gaminess so it's not off-putting, but a definite musky flavor so you know you're eating something wild, coupled with a juicy tenderness that doesn't require mastication boot camp like other game. Plus Mo was going off on how amazing Elk Camp is. Imagine. Just a bunch of interesting guys in the woods, sleeping in tents that are already set up for you, with all the amenities you need, having drinks by the fire at night. He made it sound romantic, like a scene from *Out of Africa*. My enthusiasm crescendoed. "You know what?" I said. "You only live once. I'm in."

"Awesome! Venmo me six thousand dollars."

Let's pause here to discuss hunting finances. I always assumed hunting was a redneck, poor-person sport; they like to make you think it is. Just something salt-of-the-earth dudes

---

*Nor, come to think of it, am I averse to owning a cement truck. Imagine rolling up to the club in that thing! Full disclosure: I haven't rolled up to any club in decades.
†I know, chicken tikka masala was invented in Scotland, not India. Nice try, woke police!

do. However, it is not. It's dumb expensive. It gives skiing a run for its money. First off, airfare and hotel ($800). Next, clothing. You need to buy like fifty layers of expensive synthetic garb ($500). Sweat is the enemy when you hunt. If temperatures are low, you could be in trouble with hypothermia. You're constantly removing and adding layers, so you can stay active and not sweat. These layers reside in your very high-tech backpack ($500). Throw in boots ($300) and wool socks ($40). Also, survival gear: GPS ($320), solar GPS charger ($50), water filtration kit ($40), first-aid kit with tourniquets ($120). Now to guns and ammo. Hunting rifles typically cost you $1,000. Add to that a scope ($600), a strap ($75), ammo and bullet case ($100). Don't forget the cost of processing* the animal ($300), having it shipped to you ($600), and having it mounted ($600). The price for the tag we so luckily drew was itself $650. Lastly, there is the actual Elk Camp: four days in a tent, meals, and the outfitters who guide your hunt ($5,000!). Then a tip for your outfitter ($750). We're at over $10,000 here—$12,395 for a four-day trip with minimal amenities. Makes skiing at Vail seem like a bargain.

We landed in Albuquerque with our three Hermès Birkin bags' worth of gear and were picked up by our outfitter, Hunter. His name is . . . Hunter. Hunter's vehicle looks like a monster truck on steroids. It's decked out in camo, with that intimidating metal battering-ram stuff you see on the front of trucks that makes them look mean, and as you drive by makes you say, "That guy must have a minuscule penis." To top it off, his license plate reads HUNTER. The truck looked like some-

---

*Butchering.

thing a bad undercover PETA activist would drive to fit in with hunters so he could do a hidden camera exposé about them. Taking in the scene, we tossed our gear into the truck bed and started to make our way to camp.

When you conjure up New Mexico topography, you think of desert and majestic tabletop mesas straight out of a John Ford western. And we had our mesas. Then we turned up a road at a sign that read SANTA FE NATIONAL FOREST, and not a minute later we went from arid desert to lush pine forests that seemed to have gotten lost on their way to the Pacific Northwest. Slowly, the trappings of normal life were plucked away. First the phone reception went, then the people camping dwindled to zero, then the painted road lines disappeared, then the road disappeared, and we were on a rocky dirt path to Elk Camp.

To hunt elk on public land is not an easy feat. Since everyone has access to the territory, you need to go far out to be alone. This quest for isolation is what makes hunting in the United States both beautiful and frustrating. In Europe, most hunting is private. You need to pay a ninth-generation property owner for the right to hunt on his family's land. It's usually a one-day affair: You harvest a stag that is part of a managed population under very little pressure from hunters, making him easy to stalk. Then you end up at the château drinking Bordeaux in your stylish après-hunting clothes while a child plays the harpsichord. Sounds like my dream. But this leaves most of the blue-collar European population out of the loop.

European hunting has way more of a classist element to it, and only the upper class can partake freely. In the United

States, it's way more egalitarian. Yes, we have the fancy European-style experience if you want it, but it's rare. We have public land hunts, which in my opinion are way more badass. These animals are not bred, they are as wild and wily as they come. They're under immense hunting pressure, which turns them into stealthy hide-and-seek forest ninjas. They also have more room to roam, so they're harder to find, hence you're forced to wander the recesses of our gorgeous country that few people have ever seen. And everyone who grows up under the majestic Stars and Stripes, whatever race, color, or creed, has the God-given right to hunt . . . so long as they can pony up five hundred million dollars for the gear. We bounced along the bumpy dirt road for more than an hour, as my internal monologue went from "Wow, this is so rustic" to "Are we being abducted?" At last Hunter spit his dip out the window and said the magical words we had been waiting for: "Boys, welcome to Elk Camp."

He pulled off the road and my eyes widened as I found a new me, Daniel Boone settling in to the far reaches of undiscovered America. What struck me first were the tents. These were not REI tents you put together in a clumsy ten minutes. These were shelters from a different time. They looked like housing for forty-niners panning for gold in the 1800s[*]—three big sturdy-looking white canvas tents, with four walls and a roof, resembling a Monopoly house. Each tent's roof had a copper chimney sticking out of it that was fed by a woodstove

---

[*]1849 to be exact—that's why they were called forty-niners! Because of the gold rush of 1849! Thanks, Wikipedia.

meant to keep us warm during the bone-chilling nights. Two of the tents were for sleeping, one was the kitchen, and between them was a circular firepit surrounded by chairs. This setting was romantic, rugged, luxurious for another century, nostalgic in the current one. Welcome to Elk Camp indeed.

The other hunters came out to help us unpack the car. There was Churchie, who was Hunter's father. Churchie was a little man, but he—

Oh wait. There was a fourth tent. Time to pause the story to tell you about my aversion to all things scatological. I abhor the topic. If I'm with friends and someone brings up shit, farting, etc., I will scold him and tell him never to bring up such vileness again, especially while I'm eating. If I'm watching a comedian and he starts going down that road, I will leave the comedy club for ten minutes. It's my misophonia. My sensitivity to this uncivil discourse sends me into a rage over which I have zero control. I tell you this because unfortunately I have no choice but to talk about such unsavoriness in this chapter. And I want to be clear that I am not doing this for cheap laughs. Nothing would bring me more pleasure than to leave out this next part, but it features prominently in the story. So here goes. Let's talk about . . . the shit tent.

The shit tent is a tiny tepee. You crouch to enter, and zip together behind you the plastic nonbreathable flaps. The meager four square feet of ground, hard to maneuver in, is covered by a sullied industrial rubber mat dotted with holes—the kind you see on the floors of professional kitchens. The centerpiece of this dungeon of muck is an extra-large orange Home Depot bucket lined clumsily with a black garbage bag, and perched over the bucket is a cracked hospital toilet seat. Without ventilation, the smell inside the tent assaults the nares and induces nausea at lightning speed. The garbage bag holds most of the wretchedness at the base of the bucket. However, clinging to the bag's sides are shit stalactites of different shades and textures that are impossible to avoid or unsee. Okay. That's the end of that paragraph. Excuse me while I take a shower.

Back to Churchie. Hunter's dad was a lifelong outfitter who had traveled the world guiding less-experienced hunters boldly into the wild and safely out of it. He was full of insane stories. Once he got lost driving a hunter in the mountains of Armenia during a snowstorm. They passed a second hunter, who felt that they were encroaching on his turf. Hunter number two blocked Churchie's car, got out with his buddy, stabbed two of Churchie's tires, and drove off, leaving them for dead. Churchie grabbed his axe, quickly cut down two branches, and shaped them into spikes to plug up the holes. The hemorrhaging of air stopped, and he was able to drive them to safety. Churchie taught his son Hunter everything he knew—and he better have, with the name he gave him.

Churchie wasn't quite what you picture when you think of an outfitter. He was old, short, and a little pudgy. He walked with a limp, from having had his foot run over on a hunt decades ago, and his gimpy shoulder dated from when he was fishing off a dam and fell into a tree. He was missing the top part of his forefinger because . . . why not? Churchie's body was less a temple and more a shrine to all the dumb stuff he had done in his life. His hearing was *awful*—in a profession that prizes stealth and intense listening. So though Churchie was fun to talk to, we did not want him to be our outfitter. Unpacked and exhausted from the journey, I went to smoke a cigar and relax next to the fire, under the moon. The two other hunters joined me.

Jared and Paul were old friends from western Pennsylvania, and they worked at one of the last remaining spring factories in America. Jared was dense; he emitted no light from the inside. He wore functional prescription glasses that sat on splayed ears, had a walrus mustache, and wore a camo baseball cap high on his forehead that allowed sturdy bangs to peek out underneath. He spoke about the spring factory, and springs in general, like they were God's gift to humanity. Imagine the next couple of lines spoken with the gravitas of someone recounting an Everest ascent, mixed with the cadence of Forrest Gump describing shrimp. "We manufacture all different kinds of coils. Tension springs, goes without saying. Compression springs and torsion springs, we used to do flat springs, but not so much anymore. We do constant springs, variable springs, we made serpentine springs for a time . . . cantilever springs, arc springs, volute springs. Of course, we made negator springs, but as you probably know most of that manufacturing has moved to China. Unlike the torsion spring, which, of course, we make right here. Then there's—" Jared can keep this up for fifteen uninterrupted, brutal, I'll-never-get-them-back minutes.

His buddy Paul was way less of a know-it-all. Humble, quiet, bordering on gaunt. He had no hair on his head and face, and his pallid skin suggested he had some sort of condition, but it would have been uncomfortable to ask about it. So, I have no idea, but I hope he's okay. I liked him. He was the electrician at the spring factory and would stare silently into our fire every night with an existential gaze, which made me think all was not well physiologically. Either that, or when Jared started talking springs, he too dreamed of jumping into the fire.

Jared and Paul drove all the way from Pennsylvania to New Mexico in four days. I had a "let them eat cake" moment when I asked why they didn't just fly—assuming the cost of hotels and gas would outweigh a couple of boarding passes. But they were sleeping in their beat-up F-150 in truck stops dotting the interstate and living off venison jerky from the previous season's hunt. Plus transporting the elk meat costs more than two first-class tickets. I felt stupid for asking, and my ignorance did not help me befriend what were already strange bedfellows. It also didn't help that while they were drinking Coors Light, I was sipping on biodynamic Beaujolais that I brought with me from L.A. I offered and they declined. Explaining that it was not just regular Beaujolais, but a cru Beaujolais from Mathieu Lapierre, one of the finest producers of Gamay in the region, didn't change their minds and just made matters worse.

Politics were unspoken but could be assumed. They really *hated* bureaucrats and used that buzzword often and vaguely. When they found out I lived in Los Angeles, the response was "I bet bureaucrats love it there." Huh? They hated the Department of Game and Fish, which they thought stifled their freedoms. They railed against regulations on hunting and guns, and authority in general. No, they didn't talk political leanings, but if it looks like a duck, talks like a duck . . . they'd gladly shoot the duck.

It was dark, the fire was fading, and the sky seemed dense more with white stars than the dark spaces in between. Hunter took a last sip of his beer, crumpled the can, and chucked it into the fire. Before I could say "recycling bin," he launched into the rundown for tomorrow's hunt.

"We wake up at five A.M. I'm taking Jared and Paul. Mo and Dan, you're going with Dad."

"Who's coming with me?" screamed Churchie.

"Mo and Dan."

"One more time." He was squinting, leaning in.

"Mo and Dan!"

Mo and I looked at each other, not thrilled that our leader was someone we would normally help pack groceries into his car. We headed into our tents, threw logs into the stove, and went to bed.

Before the sun peeked out, when it was still freezing outside, we arose. Breakfast was served. I'm not a big breakfast guy. On most days I have a piece of fruit with my cappuccino. If I'm feeling crazy, I'll make a smoothie of frozen bananas, wild blueberries, peanut butter, and chia seeds. I actually packed my Nutribullet, but seeing the group's reaction to my wine, and knowing the importance of breaking bread for camaraderie, I was going to eat as the crew ate. And boy did they eat. Breakfast every day was a plate overflowing with four factory-farm eggs, three strips of thick anemic bacon, a thin sinewy well-done steak, three pieces of Wonder Bread, and sad Styrofoam cups of instant coffee. I tried not to be pretentious about the meal in front of the guys, and I wasn't.* I just accepted that I would be sweating animal fat from my pores all day.

---

*Until now, I guess.

Hunter manned the propane grill. "Dan, bacon?"

"Yes, please, I'm a bad Jew."

Everyone froze. Hunter turned away from the food. "You . . . you're a Jew?"

Silence, except for the bacon sizzling.

"You're a Jew" is so much more jarring than "You're Jewish." Asking if someone is Jewish carries an air of curiosity, whereas asking if someone is a Jew suggests a response of "We found him!"

"Yeah," I said, then nervously cleared my throat. "I'm a Jew. I'm Jewish." Everyone remained frozen and made strange eye contact with one another as the bacon kept laughing. I can't really fault the guys either. They had never met a Jew before, so I'm not gonna cry "anti-Semitism." I'm going to give them the benefit of the doubt and cry "fascination with something new." Although I imagine when you see a giraffe in the wild for the first time, you don't clench up like they did. Also, my name, Dan Ahdoot, doesn't scream Jew. Ahdoot is a Hebrew word meaning "unity" that is specific to Jews from the city of Isfahan in southwestern Iran. I'm guessing they didn't know that. Mo, on the other hand, has a clearly Arabic name— Mohaned. I'm sure they weren't thrilled about him either, but at least they had enough time to prep for the Muslim. Mohaned Al-Humadi is a pretty big hint. On the other hand, I just "pop goes the weaseled" my Semitism on them.

I had to break the awkward silence with a joke. "Can we still be friends?" Hunter answered a little too seriously, "Yeah, yeah. Of course we can. Of course." *Wait till they find out I'm also Iranian,* I thought. We were still cool, but there was a palpable shift. If they weren't warm before, now they were as frigid with me as the outside temperature (and it was so cold I was wearing my fifteen-dollar hand and toe warmers).* However, we didn't have time for a breakout session on "Jews and Their Perception in Society" because we needed to start stalking.

Mo and I geared up, turned on our headlamps,† and followed Churchie into the woods—where I witnessed a fascinating metamorphosis. In the undergrowth Churchie seemed to transform before our eyes, from an old frail man into a mystical interpreter of the woods. His gait became slower, but he still somehow moved at the same pace, as if in slow motion, everything about him, his legs, his arms, the bounce of his head, even the pace of his blinking. His steps made no noise. I was supposed to be looking for elk, but I couldn't take my eyes off the creature ahead of me.

Suddenly, Churchie stopped. From his jacket he pulled out a tiny spray bottle he had filled with talcum powder. He sprayed the powder into the air, where it took the shape of what looked like a baby ghost. The ghost then disappeared, and Churchie adjusted our trajectory according to how it dispersed. You don't want the wind blowing behind you, wafting your scent toward the elk.

As we followed, Churchie translated the forest for us. He pointed his walking stick at a small footprint. "Male coyote," he whispered, "three days ago," then he walked on. Ahead he pointed to some roughed-up tree bark. "Elk rub," he declared.

---

*I'm just now realizing my money preoccupation probably isn't helping with Jewish stereotypes.
†Fifty dollars. Last one.

He touched the tree's scab with what was left of his forefinger. "About a week old," he decided. He even had comedy bits. He stuck his middle finger in a cow* patty, then stuck it in his mouth and said, "She ate eggs for breakfast." The joke being that the finger he actually put in his mouth was his index finger. Whether sticking your finger in cow shit is worth the payoff of the silly joke is highly debatable, but as a comic I respect the commitment.

We reached the end of the trees, and a huge clearing lay in front of us. This is where we would see elk if they were out. We turned off our headlamps and stopped moving, waiting in the cold for the sun to wake up. About five minutes later, with just a handful of photons gracing the field, Churchie took his janky binoculars out of a beat-up leather case. I flashed Mo a "what the fuck?" There's no way anyone in this light could see anything, let alone our geriatric tracker, but Mo and I followed Churchie's lead, with our super-high-tech binos.† I swear to you there was nothing to see. It was as if I hadn't removed the lens covers. While I scanned the black, Churchie's whisper made its way to my ears with the same pace of the talcum ghost wafting through the air. "Two bulls and a cow, four hundred yards away." I looked up at him, then at Mo, then through my lens. Lo and behold, there was the slightest speck of a different shade of dark. This, I was told, was a bull. I was, and continue to be, astonished.

Churchie put his binos away and started off in slow motion, making sure not to crumple any dead leaves under his

---

*Not moo cow. A female elk is a cow. Like, come up with another name, animal-naming people.
†Four hundred dollars. I lied.

steps. We followed behind, less like dutiful hunters now and more like disciples following their prophet. A prophet aptly named . . . Churchie.

The sun got slightly bolder, and I could see the elk in the distance with my naked eye. My heart started to beat faster; my breath became shallow. Churchie took out the talcum again, and much to his chagrin, our little ghost, as curious about the elk as we were, flew straight toward them. Churchie took out his binos. "Shit. Don't move. They're looking our way. Too far for a shot." Mo and I lifted our binos, and the three of us engaged in a staring contest with three of the most regal animals in nature. Deer picking up our scent would flinch and run off in a crisscross pattern, as if they had googled "how to run away from someone shooting you." Elk don't do that. They sensed us, the lead bull blew steam out his nose, and one by one they turned as if an invisible jockey reined their heads up high and away from our prying eyes. Though we could barely see them, we could hear the dense thud of sturdy hooves hitting the ground as they disappeared into the forest. Elk are all class. They didn't rush to seek shelter. They sauntered off because they were too good for us. It made me love them even more.

This brutal game of hide-and-seek went on for three days. Each day we would get close, spook the elk, and go in search of others. We were hiking rugged woods for about twenty miles a day in the cold. We were hungry, exhausted, shivering the whole time, mentally drained, and disheartened. I mention this because whenever I explain to nonhunters that I hunt, they scoff and say something dumb like "Oh, so you get your gun and go shoot a defenseless animal and feel like a real man?" Nonhunters think hunting is like the Nintendo video game

Duck Hunt.[*] You scratch your balls on a comfy couch and kill animal after animal until you get tired. My longest streak of never seeing an animal in the woods was seven days. Elk hunting, especially on public lands where the animal has nothing fencing it in, is exceptionally challenging. It tests you physically, mentally, and spiritually. Most people think it's not a fair fight, and they're right, but in the wrong way. A wild animal on its home turf, with its ultra-paranoid senses that have evolved to protect it from predators, is way better equipped to beat me with my flat feet, deviated septum, and astigmatism.

Three days in, and my odds of getting an elk seemed the same as if I had stayed in Los Angeles. Oh yeah, also, I had not gone to the shit tent in three days. My insides had shut down at the thought of spending a second in there, and I was totally cool with it. Not only that, I was impressed with my GI tract— good on you, you classy bag of tubes.

We came back from the third day's hunt with our tails between our legs. My post-hunt tradition had become smoking a cigar by the fire. The crisp air of the forest mixed with the warm toasty nutmeg-leather smell of a cigar was a delicious lesson in contrasts. I pulled one out, a beautiful corona called Rose of Sharon, lit it, and sat outside my tent with Churchie to hear insane stories. Mo and Hunter decided to go to a tiny piece of land about a mile from camp dubbed "the Phone Booth" because it was one of the few places in the woods you could get reception. About two minutes after they left, Churchie paused in his story of taking a centenarian named Edna on a buffalo hunt in Zambia, playfully tapped my fore-

[*] As did I, in Chapter 2.

arm, and said, "Hey, Dan, want to play a fun joke on them? I'll drive us out to the Phone Booth, and we'll be waiting there relaxing while they hike up all tired." I mean, it wasn't the best prank, but I'd be able to use my phone, so why not? Driving us through the woods on a tiny dirt road dotted with rocks, Churchie did things with his dinky, beat-up Isuzu Tracker I never imagined possible—going over tree stumps, hugging axle-wide cliffside roads, maneuvering at angles that defied physics. Ordinarily, I'd be scared shitless, but I relaxed in this old deaf dude's hands.

We arrived at the Phone Booth. It was ten square feet of land on a steep hillside blanketed by pine needles, with breathtaking views of the mountains in the distance. It felt like I was living in a Bob Ross painting. A giant tree had fallen right in the booth. I lazed on it, smoking my cigar, looking in the direction the guys would approach from. Hunter and Mo huffed and puffed their way to us, we had a laugh, then we got on our phones and caught up on all the bullshit back in the world. Five minutes later we got into the car and drove back to Zero Bars.

We sat by the fire that night. Jared talked springs, Paul stared into the fire, and everyone joked about how bizarre it was that I hadn't visited the shit tent yet. I can explain: Nobody had killed an elk yet, and there's nothing to talk about at Elk Camp until someone kills an elk. Springs would have to fill another night.

The next morning, we got up, had our hyper-caloric breakfast, washed our faces with freezing water out of those buckets they throw on the coaches when they win the Super Bowl, got dressed, took pisses, and *Groundhog Day*'d our way back into the woods. By this time, we knew the drill. See elk from afar; try to get close; they get spooked or they're cows.* Churchie decided to take us to another part of the valley to change our luck.

There comes a time in every unsuccessful hunt when you make peace with not getting an animal. Instead, you shift to appreciating the nature around you. Being in nature as a hunter is different from communing with the great outdoors as a camper or hiker. A hiker follows a well-traveled path, walking briskly, taking deep breaths, stopping for pictures, listening to music, sighing "ahhh" after satisfying gulps from their Nalgene. A hiker is an observer of nature. A hunter is a participant. Hunting is many things, but pleasant is not one of them. There's rarely a paved trail. You're walking on loose rock, twisting your ankles, through thorny brush whipping at your flesh, in brutal weather, all the while trying to stay quiet and stalk an animal who, most of the time, knows you're there. There are also stunning moments in nature that a hiker will never see—like hiding in full camo at sunrise and getting to see nature wake up when she doesn't know you're there. And that's awesome. I've seen foxes come within a few feet of me, fawns eating crab apples a stone's throw away, birds landing on my backpack. It's one of my favorite parts of hunting becau—

"SHHHHHH!"

Churchie stopped behind a tree and pointed in the distance to a huge patch of grass. A bright blond bull about a thousand yards away was charging for the valley in front of us.

---

*Shooting the female is way more regulated and requires a separate tag that is even harder to get. You see! Chivalry isn't dead.

"Chamber a round," he whispered to me. With the soprano click-click of my rifle's bolt, my kumbaya thoughts of being one with nature gave way to my reptile brain's most basic instinct—Get Food.

Out of a clearing came a spike—a small bull who doesn't have a rack yet, just a couple of spikes sticking out of its head. Since this was my first elk, I wasn't going to be picky. Churchie put down his sticks for me to rest my gun on.* I stared into the scope and rested my crosshairs just behind the elk's right shoulder, aiming for the heart and the lungs.

Now is a good time to talk about buck fever. This comes on when you see the animal, and the sight makes you shake, you hold your breath, you can't focus, you choke. I've gotten buck fever only once—the first time I saw a deer in the woods. I was in a tree stand, and a beautiful whitetail buck showed up in front of me. Hands shaking, I brought my rifle to my face, stared through the scope, and saw nothing. I pulled my head up off the scope and saw the deer right in front of me. Yet back to the scope, nothing. I thought my buck fever was so intense that my bearings must have been off and I had to be aiming at something black. As the graceful buck meandered away from me, I pulled my gun down by my side, dumbfounded until I realized I had forgotten to take the lens cover off my scope.

But that was the only time. I learned how to calm my breath

---

*Sticks are just that: two tall sticks that crisscross. Where they meet, you lay down your gun to stabilize. Most people have high-tech retractable ones. Churchie's setup was two discarded old ski poles that he duct-taped together at the pivot point. This guy was awesome.

with my mindfulness practice to become a pretty accurate shot when it was game time.*

My crosshairs relaxed, my breathing namaste, I started to count down from three when Churchie whispered, "Wait! He keeps turning back. Something's up." This was some Malcolm Gladwell ten-thousand-hour expert shit. To me, the elk was turned to the side, but Churchie saw its head at an awkward angle and its breathing energetic. It wasn't just standing still. It was looking back at something. Something big.

Then as the spike started to walk toward us, we saw a rustling in the woods behind him, slowly making its way to the clearing, until out of the trees emerged the biggest animal I had ever seen. I gasped and the hairs on the back of my neck stiffened to attention.

"Gun on the sticks." Churchie's whisper was measured yet urgent. It was the first time he addressed me less like an outfitter and more like a father. It was respectful, but admonitory: "Don't mess this up, son." The regal elk with its enormous rack took stock of the land in front of him, like Mussolini preening on a balcony to the crowd below. The spike lowered its head in deference, and they started to graze. I was following through my scope, but rather than being fixed on the target, my crosshairs were going bonkers. I couldn't still my shaking. "Take your shot," said Churchie. I heard him. The elk was 250 yards away. A couple of millimeters here or there is the difference between life and death. But my biggest hunting fear was that I would wound the animal and he would flee, only to die

---

*I'm sure this was the intention of the people who created the Headspace app.

a slow, agonizing death. "Take your shot," Churchie said, louder. Mo jumped in, "Dan, take the shot." I blinked hard, but had trouble focusing, couldn't calm my breathing. I could do nothing to break my buck fever. "I can't." I didn't feel comfortable until I had a clear shot. Mo didn't say anything, but I could feel his frustration. This bull was a trophy even for a seasoned hunter like himself. To let him go wasn't just a failure for me, but an affront to Mo.

The two elk lifted their heads briefly to chew their feed, then continued grazing. This gave me a moment to collect myself. I exhaled none too smoothly when suddenly the spike's head shot up straight to us. So did the bull's. "Shit. They know we're here," said Churchie. "You're gonna miss your chance." Mo stuttered to speak, but nothing came out. My trigger finger tremored. As the elk started to run, I kept my scope on the big bull. I wasn't going to shoot—you never shoot an animal once it's mobile. It's almost impossible to hit, and too easy to maim. Thinking I had lost him calmed my nerves in an instant. Now I was enjoying a magnificent nature show through the scope of the gun.

All of a sudden, the bull stopped and looked back at me.

I felt a pang. A weird thing happens sometimes when you hunt, where you root for the animal to get away. It's like wanting the bad guy in a movie to win. Or maybe it's just me; most of my life I *did* root for the animal and thought the hunter was evil. Now I can make a strong argument that the nonhunter who eats meat lives the more ethically dubious life. But no amount of litigating can rid me of this pang. I get it every time I see an animal in my scope. Because I thought the hunt was over, my adrenaline plummeted, and my crosshairs were stock-still behind his right shoulder. At the end of a steady exhale, I squeezed lightly on the trigger.

Boom.

All was black. I recovered from the rifle's recoil and looked up to see the elk lurch forward, a sign he was hit. But rather than fall, he regained his footing and began galloping at full speed, heading to a hill, over which I would lose him. Unbeknown to me, I was suddenly sprinting through the forest to get a better shot at him, running at full speed with my rifle in both hands like Daniel Day-Lewis in *The Last of the Mohicans*. He neared the top of the hill, and I saw a tree with a broken branch at a perfect height to rest my gun on. He was slowing down, the effects of my shot catching up to him. He stopped. I set up on the branch stub, ground my panting to a halt, and took another shot. He collapsed to the ground. Then I did the same. Out of breath and mentally drained, I slumped by the tree as Mo and Churchie approached, cracking up. "What the hell was that, Danny?" said Churchie. "You took off!" "I know!" I gasped. "I got him."

Mo helped me up and the three of us made our way to the elk. The size of him! I couldn't believe how large he was. I was struck by his dramatic transformation from king of the forest looking down upon us to the furry face against the dirt looking up at us, breathing his final breath. My eyes welled with tears. I was elated. I got my elk; he wasn't maimed; he died quickly. Mo put his arm around me, and we hugged.

We butchered the elk into quarters, and carefully removed the backstraps—two huge fillets of meat that lie on either side of the spinal column. They are the least used muscles on the animal, so the most tender. My mind was racing through a Rolodex* of potential preparations. Ooh! Elk au poivre—crusting the thick fillets with large chunks of mortar-and-pestle-ground toasted black peppercorns. Pan-searing them in butter, garlic, and thyme. Deglazing the pan with cognac, then cream. Old-school. Perfect. I snapped out of it and draped the backstraps over a tree branch, like two shawls on a coatrack, as we worked. Halfway through, Churchie left us to go get the Isuzu to pack out the meat. Mo and I finished up. Well, Mo finished up—one of the advantages of having an orthopedic surgeon on a hunting trip.

No matter how much I hunt, the butchering always mesmerizes me—how quickly an animal goes from a steaming carcass to neat cuts of meat you would buy in a supermarket with zero regard for the once-living animal. I won't get preachy about how anyone who eats meat needs to hunt to see where their food comes from—I'm absolutely guilty of being a careless carnivore. But when I eat food I've killed, it's different. I'm not quite filled with gratitude, although there is that. There's guilt, sorrow, pride, and if I'm being honest, disgust. Yet the sum is still extremely enjoyable—just complicated. The way eating another animal that was once living should be, IMHO.†

Churchie drove back and helped Mo pack the meat and the taxidermy-worthy parts of the animal while I prepared for inevitable ridicule as I fished through the gut pile. Ninety-nine percent of hunters leave the innards in the field, an amuse-

---

*Oof. I'm dating myself with that noun.
†See! I'm young and hip!

bouche for coyotes, bears, and ravens. I, however, happily joined my dining partners at this far from awful offal buffet.

"What the hell are you doing?" said Churchie, right on cue.

"Organs are the best part, Church," I replied.

"That's nasty, Dan," he said, baffled.

From the gut pile I pulled the heart, bloodied and dripping, Indiana Jones Kali Ma–style.

"I can't wait to change your mind."

For all the manliness and bravado hunters possess— murdering animals in cold blood and hacking pungent carcasses—nothing turns them into, for lack of a better expression, little bitches more than the thought of eating organs. I revel in opening the eyes of lifelong hunters to the joys of the discarded bits. While liver, kidneys, and testicles are a bit more advanced, I have yet to find a wussy woodsman not completely converted by the taste of the animal's ultimate delectable—its heart.

We arrived at camp to a hero's welcome. Hunter and the guys embraced me earnestly and helped unpack the elk, hoisting its joints on a large tree branch to dry them out. They asked about the hunt. "I'll tell you over lunch," I said, pulling the sticky heart out of a loose supermarket bag I found in the Isuzu. I walked to the kitchen tent, turning quickly to see everyone staring dumbfounded. "Trust me, guys."

My preferred method of cooking heart is sliced thin and served alongside chimichurri—an Argentinean herb sauce typically made by mincing parsley, oregano, cilantro, red pepper, garlic, and shallots in vinegar and olive oil. It adds a tangy brightness to anything, especially grilled meats. I was ready to improvise, but the closest I could get was iceberg lettuce, canola oil, garlic powder, and Tabasco. Gross. I wanted this to be special.

I locked eyes with a bottle of soy sauce, and my mind went to yakitori—the Japanese art of skewered meats. I am a yakitori fiend. Typically, you baste the meat in something called tare*—a mix of soy sauce, sugar, sake, and mirin† (rice wine). It's grilled slowly over coals, the tare caramelizing and clinging to the charring meat. It's sweet-and-savory heaven. Well, I had soy sauce and sugar. I didn't have the sake and mirin, but the alcohol basically burns off, and for a light spirit we had an abundance of Coors Light.

"Guys, start a fire!" I yelled out. I mixed the beer, soy, and some sugar—and for a little more oomph, I decided to add "the people's oomph"—ranch dressing.

Wait! Don't throw the book across the room!

My thinking was, ranch is basically mayonnaise and buttermilk, and a bunch of God-knows-what flavorings. At the Spotted Pig we would sometimes brush mayo on proteins, particularly halved lobsters, before putting them in the oven, and it was awesome.

Tare complete, it was time to prep the heart. I made an incision from the atrium, through the tricuspid valve, down to the bottom of the ventricle, making sure not to puncture the septum.‡ I then cut along the inside wall and rolled the heart out like unfurling a scroll. After cutting away vasculature and rinsing off the residual blood, it was ready—a divine, crimson tablet of lean delectable meat. I cut it into strips for skewering.

---

*Pronounced "tah-reh."
†Pronounced "mirin."
‡Finally my Hopkins education pays off.

Shit. Skewers.

There were no skewers, but there were pine trees aplenty. All the fancy-pants Nordic Michelin-starred restaurants use branches as skewers, so why not us? I cleaned up some branches, sharpened the ends, and started threading the strips of heart.

I placed the skewers into the bowl of my white-trash tare and walked out to the guys. There were no grill grates, so we were going to cook these à la s'mores. I handed each of them a pine branch and took my seat by the fire.

"I've been hunting for over sixty years, and I never ate the heart," said Churchie.

"Because you're a smart man," said Hunter, as everyone laughed.

I ignored them. "Everyone, put your skewer in at the same time as me, and take it out when I do. If heart is overcooked, it tastes like leather."

"I'd rather eat leather than heart," said Jared.

I powered through. "Ready? Go."

All six heart strips entered the flames and the tare sizzled in harmony. "Flip," I said after about thirty seconds, and my students followed. Another thirty and they were ready. I blew on the charred morsel and quickly took a bite, mostly to normalize it for my audience. The flavors blew me away. Elk, though a larger animal, is way more tenderhearted than deer. The heart was soft like a fillet, yet still had a grippy, earthy mineral tannin to it. Grilled rare, coupled with the umami-rich hobo tare, accompanied by a smooth bass note of pine, it was a magical bite. My elated silence was enough to pique their curiosity, and like dominoes each of them fell under the yakitori's spell.

Even Paul, a man of few words, chimed in with praise. My work here was done. They hearted heart.

We finally had something to talk about other than springs. Everyone huddled around to hear the tale. There's something gratifying and primitive about sitting around a fire and telling the story of a hunt. You're doing something people have done for millennia. "There's a reason early cave drawings show dudes spearing animals," my buddy Steve Rinella, renowned hunter, author, conservationist, star of *MeatEater* on Netflix, says—"it's a story we can't wait to tell."

I was on a high. I felt accomplished. A watershed moment in my hunting, this surprising activity that had become a part of my life.

Now the real story begins.

Midway through my recounting, as I was emphasizing my sudden boldness in the face of immense stress, we heard what sounded like a car approaching in the distance. We were so isolated, and this was the first car we had heard in days. The acoustics of the forest bring sounds forward minutes before you see the object itself. We turned our seats toward the dirt road, and for two minutes took guesses on who our visitor might be.

Finally, a red pickup truck raced past our camp, followed by a cop car.

"What the hell?" we thought. Was the cop trying to pull the truck over? For what? Speeding? On a dirt road? Weird. I finished the tale of my illustrious day, and retired to my tent in glory around eleven in the morning. I needed a nap.

Mo came into the tent at eleven-thirty.

"Hey, wake up."

"What's up?"

"Yo, you brought your cigar to the Phone Booth yesterday, right?"

"Yeah."

He paced before me.

"That whole hillside is on fire."

Second lurch of the day.

"What?"

"The red pickup truck driver was a hunter. He woke at five-thirty A.M., got into his truck, and went to hunt another side of the park, when he saw a whole hillside was on fire."

"What do you mean a hillside?"

"A fucking hillside!"

"How big is a hillside?"

"NOT SMALL!"

"Ohmygodohmygodohmygod."

The hunter had seen the fire and sped out of the park to get the cops—that was the race we had seen in front of us.

I started trembling. "Wait, dude, I specifically remember putting that cigar out in a way that NOTHING was left. I rubbed it out on the tree I was sitting on, then threw it on the ground and twisted a rock on top of it. I don't think it was me."

This is why Mo is such a great friend. He saw the fear inside me and knowing that no good would come from my freaking out, he agreed.

"Yeah, dude, I mean, it probably wasn't you. It's just a little weird that it's on that hillside."

"Can you stop saying hillside, please?"

Hunter came into the tent.

"Did you tell him?"

"Yeah, dude, he told me, and I don't think it was me."

Hunter wasn't as generous.

"Dan. It was one hundred percent you."

"No, man, I put out the cigar in a way that—"

"Dan. I see where the fire is coming from. I know these woods. It was definitely you."

Mo jumped in. "Well, c'mon, we don't know that for sure." But I saw Mo give Hunter a wink. Oh my god, he thought it was me too.

As Mo continued fake-comforting me, the blood drained from my face, I covered my mouth with my hand, and terror set in. I started a forest fire. Mo's voice fell into the backdrop as the voices in my head started blaring:

Dan Ahdoot. What the fuck are you doing here? You're a Persian Jew from Long Island. Your cousins are doctors and lawyers and in real estate with families and kids, but you had to buck the trend and feel unique like an idiot and here you are. You have a beautiful home in Los Angeles you could be relaxing in. Instead, you're in the forest doing redneck cosplay because your dad decided to go kosher when you were a stupid kid. And look at what happened. You lit a hillside on fire.

A HILLSIDE! THE SIDE OF A HILL! Why couldn't you be boring? Be safe? Life is complicated enough and now there's a hillside on fire because of you! Trees. Gone. Wildlife. Gone. What if you killed a firefighter? What if there's a dead firefighter who's going to have one of those formal funerals you see on the local news with bagpipes and shit, and it's all because of you! And his widow is going to talk about how great he was, and you're going to be in jail, full of guilt and cock, because you needed to feel—

"Dan!"

—*like fucking Hemingway and kill a poor elk*—

"Dan!"

—even though every fiber of your genetics screams *"YOU DON'T BELONG HERE!"*

"DAN!" Hunter shouted.

I snapped out of it, my hand still on my mouth, my eyes red and bugging out at Mo and Hunter, my breathing distorted, gone. All the symptoms of buck fever, sans buck.

"I need to turn myself in. I can't believe I did this. I need to turn myself in."

Hunter got dead serious and grabbed me by the collar.

"Nobody smokes here. You hear me? Nobody smokes here."

"I do. I did! I smoke."

"Dan. Nobody. Smokes. Here."

He let go of me and peeked his head out of the tent.

"Everybody inside."

Churchie, Jared, and Paul filed in instantly. They were clearly just outside the tent listening in. I couldn't tell what they were thinking, but I could tell they did not revel in seeing me in this state. It wasn't quite pity, but there was a discomfort that I believe wouldn't have been awarded to someone they were apathetic about.

Hunter took charge. "Okay. When the cops show up"— *When!*—"nobody smokes here, am I clear?"

All three of the guys gave a solid "yup." Their three-part harmony is a sound I will never forget. Here were four strangers who weren't super fond of me to begin with, probably had more than a teaspoon of anti-Iranian hate with a dash of anti-

Semitism, and yet they were ready to join forces to cover for me. Why? I didn't get it. I sure as hell wouldn't jump at the chance to do it for them. But here they were, all staring deeply at me with sturdy, resolute gazes. It was like the manly version of the Care Bear Stare.

"I think I should go to the cops."

Hunter jumped in. "Dan, this conversation is over. Nobody smokes here. No need to get bureaucrats involved."

Yeah, *fuck bureaucrats!*

He put his hand on my shoulder, and I almost burst into tears at the love that enveloped me. A new love I'd never experienced. In college every fraternity I tried to join rejected me, and suddenly I had a group of guys, strangers, who were willing to put themselves in danger for a fellow hunter. I had most probably committed a crime, but in the Hunter* court of appeals, my mistake was understandable and one that they would overlook. I opened my mouth to try to get the words of gratitude out when I was silenced by a sound—the equivalent of the low vibration in the glass of water in *Jurassic Park* signaling an incoming T-Rex. A car was approaching in the distance.

"Everyone out!" Jared took over. "Let's just go about like nothing's off." It was the first time he had said anything that wasn't spring related. God, how I missed his talking about springs.

Mo stayed in the tent with me for a pep talk. The rising sound of the car played an awful soundtrack.

---

*Hunter as in the sport, not Hunter the person. I know. It's a lot.

"Take all of your emotions, Dan, and stuff them down in your gut. I need you to really believe that you didn't cause the fire. You need to act as normal as possible. And no confessions because you feel bad. Everyone here is on the same page. If you start running your mouth, we're all fucked."

Mo has a way of reaching me and psyching me up. I felt empowered. I would rise to the occasion. I did what he told me to do. I took all the emotions I had—guilt, shame, regret, dread—and stuffed them into my gut like a French press. There was only one problem. My gut no longer had the room for all these emotions, given that it was full of three days of factory-farm meals and three days of avoiding release.

"Oh my god, dude, I need to go to the shit tent."

"What? Now?"

Without putting my shoes on, I sprinted out of the tent.

The car was nearing. I could hear its tread flicking rocks off the road. As the guys meandered outside their tent acting cool, they saw me sprint by.

Okay. Warning on this next section. It's rough. I feel disgusting for having written it. My poor editor, Madhulika, keeps trying to get me to take it out of the book because it's so awful she needs to stop reading midway because it makes her nauseous. "Dan, this is a food book, and suddenly I want to vomit," she says, rightfully so. However, it's accurate, and if you really want to feel the despair I was feeling at the time, you should read it. I will, however, give you an out—a Choose Your Own Adventure, if you will. The "Madhulika Version" is a less vulgar account that gets the point across, and the "Dan Version" is like you're in the shit tent with me. Choose wisely.

Madhulika Version

I relieved myself with dramatic effort. It was very unpleasant.

Dan Version

Usually, when I'm in strange bathrooms, I need a good minute or so to prep—wash hands, wipe down the seat, wash hands again, set down toilet paper, etc. For the repugnancy of the shit tent, I would need a fortnight of prep. Instead, not a split second went by from when I entered to when I pulled down my pants. About a foot before I made contact with the seat, shit screamed out of my ass with the intensity of those birthday pyrotechnics that come with bottle service at trendy clubs.* I hit the seat so violently that the momentum caused it to lean on its back two legs, the bucket angled, sloshing sewage, my legs akimbo, trapped together by my pants, feculence yelling out of my ass, hands up in the air like a crazed orchestra conductor. I was frozen in space for a couple of seconds, trying to regain my balance while simultaneously trying to aim my awfulness into the garbage-bag-lined bucket. It was the worst deleted scene of *The Matrix*. Momentum reversed, the front legs of the toilet seat landed and I grabbed the disgusting cracked plastic with my hands. A seat I would normally do everything to avoid suddenly had my fingers wrapped around it holding on for dear life. Relief. The shit tent didn't tip over. I could regroup and take in my circumstances—my bare ass on a piss-soaked chair, an olfactory assault so bad it made me retch, my bare feet on the sweaty rubber floor, a gaggle of flies cracking up at the scene, and then the worst element of the whole experience—the sound of tires coming to a stop in front of our camp.

---

*Apparently I like club references, guys.

I switched to mouth breathing and pulled my T-shirt collar, drenched in sweat, over my nose. I heard a car door open, feet hitting the ground, and the door closing. Steps were taken and then silence.

Suddenly this shit tent, the place I had been dreading for the past three days, became my sacred refuge. No amount of money could induce me to leave the humid safety of the four isosceles triangles of dirty tan plastic. All the things that had disgusted me—the visuals, the smells—suddenly soothed me. They were signs of safety. At that second, the only way anyone could get me out of the shit tent was if a hostage negotiator with a bullhorn got my mom on the phone.

"How's it going?" Hunter started things off.

"Not bad. You hear about the hillside?"

For the love of God.

"Yeah, pretty big fire, huh?"

"Yeah, I saw it this morning on the way to my spot. Ended up driving out of the mountains to get reception to call the cops."

Phew, this was the hunter, not a cop, the guy in the red pickup truck. I should've just stayed in the tent, but my curiosity got the best of me. And since getting arrested was now out of the equation, I decided to leave my Refuge of Refuse.

The guys were lined up talking to the hunter—a very tall, jacked dude in wraparound sunglasses who, frankly, looked fabulous in his well-fitting hunting clothes. Everyone's face turned toward me—clearly my crew were shocked I came out of the shit tent, and from the looks of it, they wished I had stayed in there.

The hunter finished explaining how the firefighters had battled the blaze and it was under control now, but if the winds picked up, it might spread, so he was leaving the area for safety. I then launched into the most incriminating line of questioning ever.

"Is everyone safe?"

"Seems so."

"All the firefighters are alive?"

"Uh, yeah."

"Oh thank God." It sounded like I was actually thanking him.

Before I could keep taking a trip down Incrimination Road, he saw my bull, its head and rack hanging from a huge tree.

"Wow, who got the bull?"

At a time when I wanted zero attention, suddenly everyone was pointing at me.

"Jeez, that's a great elk."

He started walking toward it, and we followed.

"How was the hunt?"

I had to walk with the hunter and show my excitement at killing the bull, all the while trying not to act like (a) I just went through the most disgusting experience of my life and (b) I lit a fucking hillside on fire. Remember when I said hunters revel in telling their hunting stories? Yeah, not this time.

Our crew decided not to evacuate, and that night we all silently sat around the fire, fueled in part by four unused cigars. I joined Paul in being lost in thought staring at the fire in front of me, almost feeling taunted by it. Every loud crack seemed to say, "This is what it sounds like on the hillside!" I felt defeated. Yes, my greatest fear, the death of a firefighter, had been avoided. But I may have ruined everyone's hunt. Jared and Paul saved up for *years* to be here and now I may have scared all the game away. I let them know how I felt, and they told me not to sweat it. When I went to piss, they even played a prank on me. Upon my return, I saw my tent covered with a yellow FIRE LINE DO NOT CROSS ribbon Churchie had picked up from the side of the road.

The next morning, as if the hunting gods were taking pity on me, every man got an elk. My guilt was pretty much absolved. In fact, I began to decide maybe I hadn't started the fire after all. Other hunters used the Phone Booth, other hunters smoke, who's to say this wasn't just an awful coincidence? Mo even helped me believe my "new truth." "Yeah, man, it could've been a wayward ember from another hunting party's fire that jumped over to that area." The Wayward Ember Theory was quickly gaining as much credibility as the Theory of Relativity and the three Laws of Thermodynamics. It became my new ethos. I believed it with every ounce of my soul.

Once I was convinced that some other scumbag was to blame, I did what every criminal apparently does—return to the scene of the crime.

"Hey, let's go up to the fire."

Note I didn't call it *my* fire. Just that random fire on the hillside. Yeah, I said it, *hillside*!

The guys looked at me, confused.

Churchie chimed in, "I don't know that's the best idea."

"Oh c'mon. Guys, it's fine. Let's go! It'll be fun. How often in life can you say you saw a forest fire from super close?"

By the looks of it, they had no desire to *ever* say that. Eventually, I convinced them and we piled into the truck and drove straight to the fire. The trail was lined with the yellow tape the guys had pranked me with. The fire department had blocked off the area, so we parked and hiked the rest of the way. When we got to the clearing, my jaw dropped. Everything, short of a few defiant trees, was singed to jet black. Here and there a few small fires still burned. It looked apocalyptic. Even Hunter and Churchie, who had been coming back to these woods for more than a decade, couldn't tell where we were because all the landmarks had been charred to ash.

We made our way toward the most adorable fire truck twenty feet in front of us. They make them really small to be nimble in the forest, so it looked like a Lego assembly. Firefighters tended to the straggling flames. One of them headed up to greet us.

"How you fellas doing?" I said with the confidence of someone very sure he didn't start a forest fire.

"Pretty good. Just about got everything under control here."

"How big is she?"

She? Like I'm an old fisherman describing a cod haul.

"About fifty acres, not that bad. We do controlled burns that are way bigger."

Relief rushed through me . . . which I shoved right back to where it came from because *it wasn't my fire to feel relief over!*

"That's good to hear. Grateful to have you guys."

I could've just left it at that. I could've been content with the Wayward Ember Theory, truly believing it, and gone my whole life telling people about how I once thought I lit a forest fire but it was some other asshole. But my dumb mouth had other plans.

"So what do you think happened?"

"Oh, someone probably didn't put their cigarette out fully or something."

Cracks in my theory started to form.

"But, like, you don't think it was started from like, a wayward ember?"

"A what?" He giggled. How dare he giggle at my theory.

Crack.

"Like an ember . . . from a fire . . . from some hunting party jumped over?"

"Ha ha, no way. There are no hunters camped near where it started. We know exactly where it started."

Gulp.

He walked us over to a World War I–size crater. In front of the crater was an X the firefighters had made with two axes. Suddenly my phone started pinging. Reception. We were at the Phone Booth.

"There was a big dead tree here, and where the X is, is where the fire started."

The X was exactly where I put out my cigar.

"I mean, you guys can't tell exactly where it started, though."

"Normally no, but this was so obvious by the depth of the crater and the char spread that we could tell."

The colossal failure of my Wayward Ember Theory tasted like dry ash on my tongue. As my fake truth died, its life flashed before my eyes: Hunter's truck at the airport, the chimney sticking out of our tents, compression springs, Churchie in slo-mo, backstraps hanging from a branch, Mo whispering to me about the fire, the yellow caution tape prank, and then the X in front of me. I was paralyzed. I swallowed, moistening my newly parched mouth. My viscera darting for hiding places in my gut, I looked up at everyone.

"Can we go back to camp?"

I don't need to tell you what happened next.

7

HELLO MY NAME IS MUMUN HELEN

FIRST-GENERATION IRANIAN AMERICANS OCCUPY AN INTERESTING place in the tapestry of American immigrants. It's very confusing for us. For thousands of years, my family has been procreating in an ancient land richer in history than most places on earth. I, however, was conceived in some studio apartment in Forest Hills, Queens. Cool. I also grew up in a country that was and remains extremely hostile to the place I come from. We've been part of the "axis of evil," of sanctioned states, of all sorts of malignment campaigns. And interestingly enough, the only people I've ever met who hate Iran more than Americans . . . are Iranians. Any Iranian who lives in America most likely escaped political or religious persecution and had no choice but to resettle, most of the time leaving everything they had worked for their whole lives back home. They fucking *hate* Iran.*

However, at the same time, you'll never meet people more proud of their heritage than Persians. They'll scream from the mountaintops about how we're the people who created the first declaration of the rights of man. Persian poetry is some of the most beautiful ever written. We gave the world the Iron Sheik! Persians love when one of our own makes it big. First female space tourist on a commercial flight? Persian. The dude who invented LASIK surgery? Persian. Andre Agassi? One of us! One of us!

But here's the sad thing about Persians—there's a good chance we'll never be able to see our ancestral homeland. The vast majority of Persians born in the United States will never go to Iran. So this land we're proud of, we boast of, is more like a mythical fantasy than an actual place. And while the history and literature of Iran are rich, that's not how most people relate to the place. We connect through the food.

Food is our only visceral link to our homeland. And Persian food is one of the most misunderstood cuisines in America. If you've never had it, you probably think it's like Arabic food. Yet we have no falafel or hummus or baba ghanoush on the menu.† In actuality, our cuisine is probably closer to that of

*The government, not the people. It's kind of like when McDonald's bought Chipotle. We all still loved Chipotle, but the parent company was gross. It's *exactly* like that, guys.

†However, we have something called kashke bademjan, an eggplant dip that makes baba ghanoush taste like spackle. Our eggplants are cooked down in an equivalent amount of onions, with a healthy heap of turmeric. They're served with fried mint and kashk, which is dairy whey, whatever the hell that means. It's white, and it brings a cool comfort to the rich, Near Eastern flavors.

India: Substitute the spices with herbs and you get Persian food. It's a cuisine less of balance and more of a struggle between flavors that are forced to play nice together. Sweet, sour, herbal, floral, earthy. The dishes are complicated, perplexing, opulent. This is not a one-pot-meal culture, nor one that comes from poverty. A lot of the best dishes in Italian cuisine came from peasants improvising with a tiny piece of cured pork and an onion. Persian food comes from the culture of royalty and excess that you'd expect from the first people to take over the world. Every Persian dinner table is stacked with enormous pyramids of heavily dressed rices, hearty braised stews, homemade pickles, and breads that give the French a run for their money.

After learning how to cook at the Spotted Pig, I realized I couldn't make one Persian dish. And so I made learning my mission. I got all the spices, the rices, the devices; I immersed myself in my culture's cuisine. And the first dish I made, probably the closest to Iran's national dish, was ghormeh sabzi.

Ghormeh sabzi is a stew of braised meat, originally done with lamb, but in the States made mostly with beef, because 'Merica.* Rather than braise the meat in a stock, you create a tea with water and more greens than physics allows to fit in that water—pounds of parsley, cilantro, chives, scallions, and fenugreek, a super-funky herb that is so pungent, not only will it smell up your apartment and the rest of the building, but you'll smell it coming out of your pores the next day.

The base of most Persian stews is turmeric and onion. You

---

*I made my version with venison I hunted, so technically this was not a ghormeh sabzi but a Bambi sabzi.

brown them together, then add anything to it—in this case, the insane amount of herbs and your meat. Then you braise the shit out of it for hours, with the added tartness of one of my favorite ingredients—limoo omani. Literally translated, it means "limes from Oman." These whole limes are baked in the sun until they're so shriveled up and dried out, they look like charred ping-pong balls and weigh about as much. But don't be fooled by their effete stature. They will tang up a stew way more intensely than a fresh lemon ever could.

An hour before it's done, you add kidney beans that you presoaked the day before. All the while, you're making rice for the base, which is an ordeal unto itself. Stay tuned. After I made this one Persian dish, I realized it would be my last. This isn't single-guy cooking. It takes three days of prep to make dinner for two. This is grandma cooking. You need to have no other job than to cook for a family of twelve, and that's where you focus your time. And nobody was better at it than my own grandma, Helen.

Mumun Helen was a jewel. She cooked a palatial meal every Friday night for fifteen to twenty people. If you saw the table she set out, you would think at least three cooks had been working nonstop all day. But, in truth, the feast was made by this one, frail, five-foot-tall-on-her-tippy-toes woman, and she spent most of the week getting it ready. She was not fast. She walked like a windup toy on its last legs. She wore a simple dress with sensible shoes—everything from Marshalls. She had wrinkles on her skin from never drinking water, only tea. She had wrinkles on her face from always laughing. She kept up with her regular "salmooni" appointments—hair and makeup. Her hands were delicate, donned with antique rings that were loose on her skinny fingers. The veins supplying blood to her constantly working hands were pronounced and thick. It was impossible to be in a bad mood when you were in her orbit because she devoted every cell in her little body to those around her. She went through breast cancer with less drama than we give to a sore throat. If an energy didn't benefit others, it was of zero interest to her.

Mumun Helen's docile, tender energy made her marriage to my grandfather, Bubu Youna, baffling. She abhorred violence and was not attracted to feats of strength or macho hubris, and yet my grandfather was the epitome of alpha male unhinged pride. If I were talking about my great-grandmother or every grandmother before her, who had arranged marriages at fourteen, a mismatch could be understood because they had no choice in the matter—the dowry decided. However, Mumun Helen was the first woman in our family to have some say in her suitor.* And she, the docile doyenne of the family, chose . . . Bubu Youna.

Bubu was the first man in Iran to own a Harley-Davidson. He hiked up mountains barefoot. He did one-handed pull-ups, cracked walnuts between his palms, and chopped huge logs with a single axe swing. When Bubu found out another suitor was at my grandmother's house, he showed up at the door with a hammer in his hand. Why my grandmother chose him is a puzzle—until you take a look at his past, and the country they grew up in as Jews.

The Jews of Iran were not a gregarious type. They were second-class citizens who tried not to rock the boat in a coun-

---

*She got married at eighteen, which for the time was old, like fifty-five.

try that didn't welcome them. Although it was better to be a Jew in Iran than in Europe, it was no walk in the park. My grandfather often told a tale from his childhood that doubled perfectly as his origin story. When he was a little boy, the ice cream shop wouldn't serve him ice cream in the stainless steel cups they gave the Muslim kids. Because he was Jewish, he was served the scoop in his hands, so as not to sully the silverware. He had to finish his ice cream fast so his hands wouldn't freeze. Sometimes, because his hands were numb, or he couldn't handle another brain freeze, he had to throw the scoop on the grass and watch it melt through his tears.*

The situation presented young Bubu with a choice: Stay in line with the other Jews and accept the way things were . . . or toughen up and become a bad motherfucker.

Bubu became a bad motherfucker.

My grandfather joined a zoorkhaneh, a traditional Persian gym that Jews *never* joined, and got as strong as his Muslim counterparts. Then he joined a boxing gym where Jews weren't welcome. Instructors there viciously beat him to make the Jew quit. Instead, he worked twice as hard and became one of the best boxers in the gym. He befriended cops and gangsters. This is not what Jews did in Iran—I mean, it's not what Jews do anywhere! He devoted most of his life to toughening up and proving that Jews didn't have to be meek followers. To my sweet little grandmother, who came from a respectable, docile,

---

*Okay, I know this is a weird time for a footnote, but let's talk Persian ice cream! The Persians were among the first civilizations to make ice cream, and it's *delicious*! It's saffron ice cream that's bright yellow. The cream in Persian ice cream is so full of fat it remains solid at room temperature, so you can actually see cubes of it within the ice cream. The white cubes of milk fat combined with pistachios make this ice cream look like golden mortadella. It's sweet, savory, and ultrarich. It's heaven in a cup . . . but not in your hands.

bookish family, Bubu must have been a breath of fresh badass air. She was well educated and spoke fluent French. He never finished high school. She came from a highly respected white-collar family in Iran, and he was from a family known more for brawling than for book smarts. She was saffron, and he was turmeric. Regardless, shortly after he showed up at her home, hammer in hand, they got married.

My grandfather worked in the Tehran bazaar, selling fabrics. The bazaars were viciously anti-Semitic. When he would order tea, they'd serve him in paper cups instead of glass. It was ice cream all over again. While other Jews in the market accepted the status quo and quietly grew their businesses, he couldn't. He never backed down from a fight, which eventually made it hard for him to conduct business, and he went bankrupt. He didn't want his children and his grandchildren to live in a world where they had only two choices—be proud and fail, or be meek and get by. So he decided to start a new life in America. While many Persian Jews in America had taken a good amount of money to the States to start a new life, my grandfather had nothing. He worked in Rhode Island at a foundry pouring melted lead into molds. It was backbreaking work, and at nights he moonlighted for a bookie in Boston, playing backgammon in smoke-filled rooms against white people who didn't stand a chance.

While he planted roots in America, my grandmother was left alone in Iran to raise three children. For three years, my grandmother had no husband by her side. This was before FaceTime and unlimited calling plans. This was a time of postcards. She took on the challenge for the greater good of the family, living in a two-bedroom apartment with her children. My uncle chokes back tears when he speaks of hearing my grandmother cry herself to sleep many nights when she thought the kids were dead to the world. During the day, however, she worked tirelessly, cooking a fresh elaborate meal for the family every night. Cooking is what kept her grounded during these awful times. Eventually, my grandfather's pride and toughness paid off and he saved up enough money to bring the family over to the States to start a new life.

In America came grandkids, and my grandmother's cooking transitioned. The meals that kept her grounded in Iran now connected her with us in America and connected us to our heritage. This is part of the reason she went all out.

Mumun Helen's dinners were a master class in Persian cookery. Let's start with the rice. Three kinds of rice were a minimum. I'm not talking white, brown, black. I'm talking rices that take an inordinate amount of preparation and that can stand on their own as meals.

Actually, let's take a moment to discuss the insanity that is Persian rice.

First, the basics of cooking it. This ain't no "throw it in the rice cooker" substance. Persian rice is always basmati, and it never comes in slick packaging. It comes out of a burlap sack that looks like it was unloaded from a UN truck deployed to some famine-ravaged place. You need to wash the residual starch off the rice so the grains don't stick together. Persians *hate* sticky rice. In fact, when we kids went to Chinese restaurants, my mom would scoff at the rice: "Crazy. These Orientals can't wash the rice for two seconds?"* But it takes a lot

---

*It was a different time.

longer than two seconds to wash the rice. It takes about three minutes of nonstop, faucet-at-full-blast rinsing to get the starch off. If Persians could be okay with sticky rice, there would be no worldwide water shortage.

Once it's cleaned, the rice is boiled in a pot of water until it's al dente. Then it's poured into a colander and, you guessed it, *rinsed off with more water!* Then it's put back in the pot with a healthy helping of oil or butter (more on this in a minute) and a very specific ratio of, hmm, I'm forgetting, oh yes, *water!* And then it's cooked with a towel underneath the lid, so that the steam doesn't condense and drop back into the rice. After the right amount of time, your rice is done. And it only took seven hours plus a kiddie pool's worth of water.

What distinguishes Persian rice from that of most other cultures is that it's rarely served just as is. Sometimes it is, as a base for stews, but rice can be its own dish when mixed with other goodies. Adas polow is rice with lentils, raisins, dates, orange zest, and saffron. Rice with fresh fava beans, cardamom, cinnamon, and a ton of dill is baghali polow. There are even sweet rices. Shirin polow has slivered orange peel, carrot strips, pistachios, almonds, and orange blossom water. These more intricate rices will double or triple the time it takes to make this base dish. And depending on whether beans have to be presoaked, this could be a two-day affair for what is in essence a side dish.

But that's not the end of the story. Let's get back to the oil and butter of it all. There's a thick layer of fat on the bottom of the pot of rice, cooking at a ridiculously low heat. It's not quite frying but almost poaching the rice. It creates a golden crust called tahdeeg, which literally translates to "bottom of the pot." Crispy rice at the bottom of the pot is not a new thing. At the bottom of the paella pot lies socarrat. At the bottom of Korean bowls lies their version, called nurungji. Now, I don't want to sound disrespectful at all, and I write this with humility. But those cultures' crispy rice can suck it. While there's a limp layer a couple of rice kernels deep, which tastes more like a stale rice cracker than anything, tahdeeg is about a half-inch-thick slab of golden crusty rice that's been simmered in fat to ethereal crispiness.

But wait. There's more!

There are tahdeeg sub-genres. There are versions of tahdeeg where you dot the bottom of the pot with sliced potatoes, creating what can only be described as hash browns from the gods. Or with lavash, a thin bread that crisps up alongside the rice. Even sliced onions have a place at the bottom of the pot. It's the best expression of crispy crunchiness that exists in the food world, in my opinion.* Ask any non-Persian who's eaten Persian food what their favorite dish is and I guarantee you it'll be tahdeeg.

Back to Grandma's table.

So you had three to four rices, and there were different braises to go with them. Ghormeh sabzi, a favorite for me and my brothers, always made an appearance. The rest were a rotating cast of characters: gheymeh, a tomato-based stew with split peas and stewed beef; karafs, a braise with sautéed celery, mint, and lamb; bademjan, another tomato-based braise with meat and collapsed eggplants; and beh, a quince-based braise with saffron and split peas. Gondi was always on the menu.

---

*Yes, including you, fried chicken.

These delicious meatballs were made with ground veal, chick-pea flour, and cardamom, gently poached in a bath of chicken broth, and served with lavash and herbs. Gondee is a food specific to Persian Jews. And I know the term "Jewish food" rarely elicits a positive Pavlovian response, but Persian Jewish food, and Middle Eastern Jewish food in general, is different. Please indulge me in a little culinary anti-Semitism.

Ashkenazi Jews, the Jews of eastern Europe, are commonly associated with an awful food culture. My theory is that it's because they were surrounded by eastern European Christians, and that's the food culture they started from. And let's be real, the Czech Republic, Poland, and Belarus have never been culinary bastions of the world. Their food can be described in two words: breadline vibes. Plus, these food cultures prominently feature one ingredient—the pig. Pork is in almost every dish; it hangs in the windows of restaurants and butchers. Pork is also the most feared object in any religious Jew's life. All this pork staring at them everywhere they went must have been so triggering for Jews that their number one priority in creating a cuisine was not deliciousness—it was to avoid swine. It's a fear-based cuisine. How good can a cuisine be when its raison d'être is avoiding certain foods?*

Jews of the Muslim world didn't suffer the same culinary fate as their Ashkenazi brethren. First off, Middle Eastern food was full of flavor, spices, and explosiveness. Also, like Jews, Muslims were scared shitless of pigs, so no pigs were hanging in windows to freak people out. The main difference is the fat used in cooking. Muslims use a lot of butter. Because

---

*See veganism.

of Jewish dietary laws, meat and milk can't be mixed together, so we substitute olive oil in many of the dishes. And frankly, one isn't better than the other. They're both delicious—oil makes dishes more savory; butter makes them more decadent. So rather than come up with a completely different cuisine, the Jews made some minor tweaks and kept the culinary culture alive and well. Sorry, Ashkenazis, it's true. Your food sucks. But hey, at least you win all those Nobel Prizes.

Mumun Helen's table was so full of food, there was barely room for plates. In fact, some nights the dinner table would act as a buffet and we'd fill up our plates and go off to our corners to eat. Mumun Helen would always ask her kids and grandkids what we thought of her food, genuinely excited to know. When she got to me, I'd love to give her a specific: "The amount of cardamom in the gondi was spot-on." I learned some of the Persian words for random ingredients, the best of which is cardamom, which in Farsi is pronounced "hell." Her passion for my notes made me want to give her more random observations. I'd say things like "The limoo omani in the ghormeh sabzi was just enough to complement the earthiness of the shanbalileh [fenugreek]," and she would light up. "Who taught you how to say shanbalileh?" And she would laugh with her whole little body and playfully slap me on the leg. We had a special bond, and it was all because of food.

My grandfather and I also had a special food bond. Though Judaism played a huge role in his leaving Iran, he wasn't very religious. Probably because he didn't like other people telling him what to do, even if the person was God. Once he was ranting about kosher laws—this at a time when I was not kosher, unbeknown to my family. I saw an opening and told him,

"Bubu, I'm not kosher." He leaned in. "I'm not kosher either!" He told me how he used to eat nonkosher food when he worked in New York City. But now that he was in a wheelchair and home all the time, he hadn't had shrimp in years. So I made it my top secret tradition to once in a while take him to eat shrimp. He loved shrimp at Chinese restaurants, but he didn't want to have it in Great Neck for fear of community members seeing him. So I'd put him and his wheelchair in my car, and we'd drive to the town over, Port Washington, and have a secret affair with crustaceans. Nothing special, just shrimp with cashews, but *man,* it knocked his head back. He even gave our secret dinners a name—"Nevelah Terefah," which basically means "not kosher" in Hebrew. He'd call me: "Hey, what are you doing? I'm in the mood for some Nevelah Terefah." Relatives didn't know of our secret dinners until after my grandfather died. And my parents are reading about it right now for the first time. *I have no regrets!*

My grandma relished feeding anyone who was close enough to her. When we'd finish dinner, enough food was left on the table that it looked untouched. She'd then start filling up immigrant Tupperware—this was anything that had once been a vehicle for something else. In a cabinet in the kitchen, she ran a rescue for discarded jars and packaging of any kind. After filling up a Dannon yogurt container with rice, and an oversize Kirkland pickle jar with khoresht, she'd call the doorman of the building to come up and collect. She'd pack enough food for him and his staff. Then neighbors in the building were called to pick up their rescue containers. The joy it brought my grandma to feed us was palpable in her permagrin.

A dark day for poor Mumun Helen came when at the table

my youngest cousin, Josh, exclaimed in what seemed like slow motion, "I hate Persian food. Why can't we have pasta?" "You don't like my food?" She didn't say it meanly. She was sad. "Pasta is just so much better," he said. I could see my grandmother's eyes well up. "Okay, I'll give you pasta next time." After that, my cousin Josh would have a side of Helen's version of spaghetti bolognese every week. It was good, but the contrast with her masterfully crafted dishes was sacrilegious. It would be like going to the French Laundry and asking for mozzarella sticks.*

Mumun Helen and Bubu Youna accomplished a lot. They started a large, loving family. They brought them to a strange new land for greater opportunity. And they carved out a nice living for themselves. What they did not have, unfortunately, was a loving marriage. Bubu Youna didn't know how to show love to Mumun Helen. He showed immense love to his kids, his grandkids, and his friends. But there were rarely if ever any "I love yous" between Grandma and Grandpa. My grandfather, like most alpha males, put so much stock in his physical prowess that as age took its toll on his physicality, he became a cantankerous lone bull, exerting the little power he had left on the only thing he could control—Mumun Helen. And it breaks my heart because I know how much my grandmother would have welcomed unconditional love with open arms. I don't know if Bubu didn't know how to show love, or didn't care to in public because he thought it made him look weak, but he didn't—except when it came to her food.

---

*Josh has since become a very successful therapist, and I'm *hoping* this behavior of his is a recurring regret that he will forever try to work out with his shrink.

This man who never said "I love you" was powerless when under the spell of Mumun Helen's food. He exclaimed with bravado that Mumun Helen was the best Persian cook that ever existed. One dish in particular, called deezee, was the closest thing that came to his love language. Deezee is Persian truck driver food—as manly as it gets. No surprise that this was my Bubu's favorite dish. Lamb is stewed with turmeric, saffron, and limoo omani. Beans and potatoes are added. Once everything is cooked, the meats and beans are separated from the broth and mashed down using a mortar and pestle into a meaty paste that's served alongside a bowl of the rich broth. Breads, herbs, and raw onions join the party. It's Persian comfort food, it's delicious, and one serving will make you succumb to the most delightful of food comas. It was always baffling to see my grandfather eating Mumun Helen's deezee because he would suddenly transform from Robert De Niro in *Raging Bull* to Ryan Gosling in *The Notebook*. Each succulent bite was followed by a barrage of compliments my grandmother would relish, while we sat on the sidelines, mouths agape.

I remember coming to Shabbat dinner once and seeing Mumun Helen's hands shaking as she brought a stew to the table. Some poured out on the tablecloth. My mom asked her what was going on, and she said she didn't know. She was soon diagnosed with an awful neurological disorder that wreaked havoc swiftly. By the end of the year, her hands were shaking with such fervor that it was impossible for her to cook. The loss was devastating to her. None of her grandkids' Farsi was that great. We communicated with her through food. And now that language no longer existed. She died shortly thereafter, and I'm sure that her inability to connect with us and my grandfather played a large role.

And with her passing went our only tactile connection to our homeland. This is not to say that none of our mothers cook—they're all amazing chefs.* Even my younger cousin Debbie (Josh's much smarter older sister) has become quite the Persian cook. But it will never be the same. Mumun Helen fed us with the fervor and passion of someone desperate to relay a story before it was too late. It's as if she knew that she was our last link between Iran and America, and she was going to give everything in her soul to make it last.

Her cooking was so vital to us that in my older brother's last few weeks on earth in the hospital, he requested Grandma's ghormeh sabzi. However, the acid from the limoo omani was so strong it burned his throat, which had been scarred from the chemo. My mom's heart was so broken by this that she still hasn't touched ghormeh sabzi, more than twenty years on. Food in our family is more than just sustenance. It holds memories, joy, pain, family, heritage, and heritage lost.

My grandfather died a few months after my grandmother. It was sad, but also strange. He had no particular health issues, and on the surface theirs was not the idyllic relationship where one person can't live without the other. But that's exactly what happened. My mom would cook my grandmother's greatest hits for Bubu, but he had no interest. His gregariousness faded,

---

*Persian men don't cook. I just might be one of the few on the planet—hence why they gave me a book deal.

and all that was left was a sorrowful mantra he repeated softly to himself with eerie frequency: "There is no light in this home anymore."

My grandfather was a slave to his pride. It was his pride that gave him the balls to court my grandmother, someone way out of his league, hammer in hand. It was his pride that didn't let him play nice with the bigots in the bazaar. It was his pride that had him leave his family behind to start over in a country he knew nothing about. It was also that pride that stopped him from being vulnerable and loving to my grandmother. But as tough as he was, and as much as he scoffed at public displays of affection, he literally couldn't live without her. Their relationship was a lot like the cuisine that acted as one of their only connections. It wasn't in balance, the flavors in a lot of cases shouldn't have worked together, but regardless, they came together beautifully.

After Mumun Helen passed, I was helping to empty her kitchen, and in the pantry I noticed that all of her spice jars were labeled with a "Hello my name is" sticker and the name of the spice written in Farsi. I assure you this was done unironically. I'm sure there was a sale on these stickers at the 99-cent store and that's how they got there.

Hello my name is لـه (cardamom)

Hello my name is شنبلیله (fenugreek)

Hello my name is سماق (sumac)

In hindsight, the stickers made perfect sense. The herbs and spices that she used to speak to all of us were indeed her best friends. They gave her purpose, meaning, and love.

8

CREAM OF TARTAR

THE FIRST THING I EVER COOKED WHEN I WAS A KID WAS A SOUFFLÉ. I know, ambitious. My mom is a tag sale maven and had bought what still remains one of my favorite cookbook series ever written, the twenty-seven-volume Time-Life Foods of the World. Leafing through the pages as a kid took me on a magic carpet ride through food bazaars in Morocco, fish markets in Tokyo, home kitchens in China. It was *magical*. The foods were so vibrant, different from anything I had ever seen. This was before everyone with a headshot was given a food travel show. However, I kept going back to one place, and one recipe, that mesmerized me.

In the book *Cooking of Provincial France,* I found the recipe for Grand Marnier soufflés. They looked so strange. A mushroom cloud puffing out of a huge ramekin.

"Mom, what's this?" I asked.

"That's a soufflé. It's very fancy. French people eat them."

"Can I make it?"

"They're very hard to make."

"Well, Mom, hard is my middle name." I was ten; I didn't get the double entendre.

So we went to the supermarket and got all the ingredients. There weren't a lot of them. We had most of them in the house—eggs, Grand Marnier, an orange, sugar. The only ingredient we lacked was something strange, a name I'd never heard before—cream of tartar.

Cream of tartar is not a cream. Nor does it have anything to do with tartar sauce. It's actually a by-product of winemaking—a powder scraped off the barrels. In baking, it's used to create fluff. Why do they call it a cream? Fuck if I know. But me and my immigrant mom were in the dairy section of Associated Supermarket scanning for cream of tartar. Finally, a "had it up to here" employee pointed us in the right direction. "It's in the spice section. Next to cumin."

"What is a cream doing next to cumin?" my mom asked. Rightfully so. And this dickhead responded, all pissed, "It's not a cream. It's a powder," then walked away. My mom gave me a look like "Remind me why we came to this country?"

We bought the cream of tartar, and I retired to the kitchen with my cookbook and ingredients, a mad little unibrowed scientist ready to get to work. First, I separated the yolks from the whites. Actually, my mom did this—although she was excited for me to try baking, the prospect of wasting dozens of eggs held no joy. That done, I added orange zest, Grand Marnier, and sugar to the yolks. My mom let me taste the Grand Marnier. It was *super* strong. "Ew!" "Don't worry," she said. "The alcohol will cook off when you heat it."

I cooked over a bootleg bain-marie, which is basically a double boiler. Direct heat on the eggs will scramble them, so you whisk them over the steam from simmering hot water. I loved stepping up to the challenge. The eggs turned pale and thick but did not scramble. Mission accomplished!

The next step was whisking the egg whites into what the cookbook called "stiff peaks." I had no idea what this meant, and neither did my mom. Again, this was before YouTube; if you didn't know how to do something, you just winged it. I put the electric whisk in the bowl for about three minutes and the whites got frothy. Then I added the cream of tartar. Suddenly, the texture of the egg whites started to morph from a limp foam into a dense cream. My eyes widened in shocked delight. Then the whisk started leaving concentric circles in its wake as the texture changed again, this time to whipped cream.

I freaked out. "Mom! Come!" She came running. "What's wrong?" "Look!" "Oh my god." We were mesmerized. When I stopped the whisk and pulled it out, I noticed a little Matterhorn in the bowl.

"That's the stiff peak!" It looked delicious—exactly like silky whipped cream. I had to take a taste. I dipped my finger in, took a dollop, and put it in my mouth. It was . . . disgusting. It was as if an egg white went into a steam room, wiped off with a towel, and I sucked on the towel. How could something look so tasty and taste so awful?

Next, we had to "fold" the egg whites into the yolk mixture.

Four pictures showed a spatula smoothly going through the mix, creating a yin and yang of yellow and white that wasn't quite uniformly combined. The whole point was not to mix too vigorously so you didn't lose the air in the egg whites. That's what gives you the rise. I took folding *very* seriously, as if a bomb would go off if I mixed too vigorously.

"You think that's enough?" I asked my mom.

"I have no idea."

We didn't have a proper soufflé dish, so I buttered the inside of a cake pan and added sugar, rolling it around to make sure every single crystal had butter to stick to. It looked like sugar Velcro. I then poured the mixture inside. Creamy, foamy, it looked delicious, but I was too dismayed by the stiff peaks to test it out.

I placed the pan in the oven and stood plastered to the glass. Imagine one of those grainy oven windows from the eighties with a shitty lightbulb that gave you only the faintest sense of what was going on inside. I waited to see if my science experiment worked.

Then, in slow motion, I saw the mixture start to rise over the lip of the pan.

"Mom! Come here!"

She ran over and we stared, entranced by what was happening.

"It's working!"

"I can't believe it," she said.

Once we pulled it out, the soufflé looked exactly like the picture in the book, except in a cake tin. A glorious mélange of pale white, light yellow, and crusty orange—like a Grand

Marnier Canyon in food form. It smelled heavenly—a refreshing, warm, sugary, steamy orchard.

"I think we need to eat it before it falls."

We brought our spoons to our sweet, spongy Frankenstein and took a bite.

Still too hot, so we ate it with our mouths open, steam pouring out. The flavor, though, was exquisite. A soufflé doesn't hit you over the head with power; it subtly lulls you in. The texture is warm silk; the taste is sweet candied yolks that have been caressed by orange. It disintegrates in your mouth quickly, and the remnants of the orange liqueur tingle your throat as a final goodbye. My mom and I were hooked. She promised to get me my very own soufflé dish . . . when there was one available at T.J. Maxx.

The soufflé became my signature dish. I made it every time my parents had company over and ended up perfecting the recipe. I no longer needed the cookbook. It was the first thing I ever cooked, and it remains my favorite dessert.

After college, I moved to New York City to pursue stand-up comedy.* This was a rough time in my life. My family was universally panning me as a delusional dipshit for graduating from Johns Hopkins with honors in premed and giving up medicine to tell dick jokes. I took a day job doing ad sales research—number crunching; a trained monkey could do it—so that at night I would be free to do open mics at comedy clubs. But the only way I could get any stage time was by barking in exchange, handing out flyers during the day to passersby

---

*I know. Awful segue. Trust me, it'll make sense soon.

all over town. Barking is degrading. Ninety percent of the people walking by you ignore you, and most of the 10 percent who stop you don't want to interact with. Add to that, I was getting almost no laughs onstage. I was committed, and I kept at it, but my confidence was at an all-time low.

That wasn't the case for my two best friends from Hopkins, Mohaned and Tiki. Mo is traditionally handsome, an Arab George Clooney doing an orthopedics residency, something he had dreamed of his whole life. He brimmed with confidence. Tiki was also doing a dream residency, in cardiology. Tiki looks nothing like an Indian George Clooney, but his mirror must tell him otherwise, because that's how he carries himself.* Mo and Tiki were handsome, charming, and doing what they loved. Their confidence was through the roof.

We would go out all the time; here's how it usually went. I'd pick a restaurant, they would pick a bar, they would leave with two girls, and I would stumble to Mamoun's Falafel alone. Rinse. Repeat.

One night at a club in Manhattan's Meatpacking district, we were chatting up three girls. I could tell the third girl was talking to me only because her friends liked my friends. She was jumping on the love grenade. At four in the morning the lights of the club came on, and Mo and Tiki planned their exit. The girls had a little confab, whispered to one another, looked back at me, whispered some more. The third girl looked pissed— her friends were leaving her. They grabbed Mo and Tiki and walked out.

---

*I set Tiki up with his lovely wife, buying me the luxury of giving him shit for the rest of time.

"Okay, I'm going home," she said.

"Wait," I said. "Would you like to . . . come back to my place for a drink?"

"I don't think so. Unless you have coke?"

"Coke? You want coke?"

"Forget it."

"No wait! I have coke."

I didn't have coke. But in the moment I saw an opening and took it. It was stupid. I should've just said, "Oh, I'm not good enough on my own for you to come back for a drink? You have to literally be drugged to hang out with me? Goodbye."

But I was so lonely and desperate then that I was willing to do what it took. My apartment was ten blocks away. I had ten blocks to get cocaine.

I texted a finance buddy who did coke. I know, oxymoron.

"Dude! I need coke. Can you help me?"

"I'm all out. I could use some too. Let me know if you get any."

Damn it! Three blocks away. I texted a weed dealer I knew.

"Hey Terry, I need some coke."

"Wrong number."

The next time I saw Terry, he gave me a *very* stern talking-to. Rightfully so. Weed dealers and coke dealers differ, apparently. One goes to Phish concerts. The other carries guns and stuff.

One block away now. I was debating coming clean, but before I knew it, we had arrived at my door.

We took a seat in my living room. I was hoping she'd forgotten about the coke, and we could just have some drinks, but as soon as she hit the couch, she said:

"So . . . Where's the coke?"

"The coke. I will get the coke . . . for us . . . right now."

Because my tiny studio apartment hid only my minuscule alcove kitchen, I scurried off there to figure out what to do. My back against the fridge, I looked up at the fluorescent light and sighed.

"What the fuck are you doing?" I thought. I wanted to flee, leaving her with the keys because I was never coming back.

"Everything okay?" she said.

"Yeah! All good, just . . . forgetting where I put the coke. Be there in a second."

I started to open and close cabinets for effect when I suddenly locked eyes with on old friend.

Cream of tartar.

Earlier in this chapter I mentioned a lot of the properties of cream of tartar—its baking uses, how it's made. What I forgot to mention is this. It has the *exact* same consistency as cocaine.

I grabbed a plate and hurriedly put out some cream of tartar, took out a credit card, and divided it into four lines of fauxcaine. I stared at the plate, shook my head, and walked into the living room with a smile.

"Here we go. Here's the cocaine you requested, m'lady."

What?

Putting the plate down before us, I looked at her apprehensively to see if she was convinced.

"Okay, you go first," she said.

"Right, okay, I'll go first."

As I slowly rolled up a dollar bill, I prayed. I had picked the cream of tartar for its texture but had *no fucking clue* what it could do to me.

I had never snorted a line of anything, let alone cream of tartar. And now I was about to inhale forty soufflés' worth. Time to turn these neurons into stiff peaks.

I snorted the line and shot my head up from the plate, awaiting some sort of reaction. Nothing happened . . . for about three seconds. Then as I handed her the dollar, I started to sneeze. Uncontrollably. Convulsively. It was bizarre. I had to hold on to the armchair. My pelvis thrusting forward with every explosion, it was more like an exorcism than a sneeze.

Then it stopped. "Are you okay?"

"Yeah I'm f—"

And again the bursts, four, five, six times. It stopped again. I opened my eyes, confused and sinus exhausted, to see her heading down to the plate with the dollar bill in her nose.

"Wait! Wait!"

"What's wrong?"

"It's not good cocaine."

"That's okay; even bad cocaine is good. It's like pizza."

"No. It's not cocaine. It's . . . cream of tartar."

"What? It's powder."

"No. Cream of tartar isn't a cream, it's a powder used in baking. A by-product of winemaking. I'm sorry. I didn't have cocaine."

"You lied about having cocaine?"

"Yes. I'm so sorry. I'm really stupid. I just got caught up at the club. I'm really sorry."

She started to laugh.

"You just fucking snorted baking powder?"

"No, it's cream of tartar."

"Why the hell do you have cream of tartar?"

"Because I like making soufflés."

We both started to laugh.

"I love soufflés," she said. "You should've offered that instead of drinks."

"Oh my god, do you want a soufflé? I'll make you the best soufflé right now."

"Hell yeah, I want a soufflé."

And at five in the morning, we drunkenly scarfed down the eggy goodness. Mo and Tiki might have been handsome and had great jobs—but I had Grand Marnier soufflés.

9

CHASING
DEAR

MY FRIEND GINGER IS AN ACTRESS IN L.A. WHO COLLECTS PEOPLE.
She has an eclectic group of friends, and when you're lucky
enough to get invited to one of her soirées, you don't say no.
She had started dating a new guy and invited eight close
friends to meet him. As we all took our seats at the table in the
restaurant, I sat across from a stunning woman named Katie.
After exchanging pleasantries, we shared a furtive whisper ap-
ropos of the elephant in the room. Ginger's new boyfriend was
Jim Carrey, and we were all expected to act like he was just
another dude.

Jim and Ginger sat at one end of the table, and Katie and I
were on the other. We weren't in earshot and could talk freely
about how awkward and bizarre the evening was. We ordered
drinks, mine a Pinot Noir, hers a glass of champagne. I re-

member thinking what a classy move that was, on a Monday no less. It was a pebble in the remarkable mosaic of this woman that was being assembled before me.

Katie is a classic beauty. Bountiful blond hair tied up loosely, the color of wheat in full sun. Her eyes are a staggering shade of hazel I didn't know existed in nature. She wore a burgundy silk camisole with delicate lace trimming, a distressed jean jacket, form-flattering leggings, and simple black heels. Although her smile was warm, she wasn't trying too hard to become friends with anyone at the table, including me. She kept her guard up, and when she let any of me in, the rush of endorphins turned me into a bumbling idiot. "Where are you from, Dan?" "New York. Well, Long Island. Which is technically New York. But yes, New York. Also, Iran. Before." That type of stuff.

I also didn't recognize her. When someone at the table gushed about a show she had acted in, I realized she was a famous actress—adding to her mystique and explaining the wall she built around her. We chatted and I was enthralled. I always struggle relating to people about work, and I get weird especially in front of famous people, so at first, I retreated. But as people around us tried to fill the vacuum, I did what I always do when I'm at a loss for words. I went to my happy place.

"So, Katie, what restaurants do you like?"

She started talking and lit up because I knew all the ones she mentioned. She had lived in New York for a while, and we loved a lot of the same places. We were locked in, talking about dishes that brought us back to places and times. I laughed inside because I had turned forty the week before and celebrated by sending an email to everyone I knew telling them I was ready to settle down, and to please introduce me to anyone they saw fit. It was a funny email that went somewhat viral, and I had about ten dates on the books. I was about to cancel all ten.

And then the waiter came over and fucked everything up.

"May I take your order?"

"Yes, please. I'll have the short ribs."

"You got it. And you, miss?"

"I'll have the scallops."

"Power move," I said.

She smiled at me, then looked back at the waiter with dead seriousness.

"Also, there's no gluten in that dish, right?"

The word "gluten" echoed in my brain. This wasn't a stone in her mosaic. This was a wrecking ball smashing the whole thing to pieces.

I know some of you readers are thinking, "So what? She's eating it—why should it make a difference to you?"

I hear you. I really do. And I wish I could get on board, but . . . humor me.

After my brother died and my parents became strictly kosher, whenever we went out, dietary restrictions, something I rarely thought about, were suddenly the *only* thing that mattered. My father asked, "Is this made with chicken stock or vegetable stock?" so often I'd wish he had it tattooed on his forehead.* In restaurants my mom cooked up fake food aller-

---

*I know. Jewish cemetery. Fine. Sharpied on his forehead.

gies: "I'm allergic to shellfish. I will die if I get shellfish." I listened, knowing full well that one of her favorite foods growing up was shrimp.

Once my dad found bacon bits in his mac and cheese and spat it out on the plate, yelling at the waiter as if he'd been poisoned with cyanide. All the while, at age sixteen, I was rebelling *against* what I saw as fake stupid rules that were hamstringing chefs, when all I cared to experience was their authentic expression of the ingredient.

Dealing with dietary restrictions coming from religion is tough enough. Then I moved to L.A. and faced a whole new host of dietary restrictions imposed by a force way more sinister than religion—vanity. Every poor menu item in L.A. sits on a bed of fresh parentheticals: (PB) Plant Based. (V) Vegetarian. (P) Pescatarian. (SP) Spicy. (PL) Paleo.* (DEBAAIWMYB)— Don't Eat Before an Audition It Will Make You Bloated.

Also, I never heard anyone talk about feeling bloated until I moved to Los Angeles. "Oh, I can't eat X because it makes me bloated." "Oh, if I even *look* at Y, I'll get so bloated." You're digesting food. You're supposed to feel heavier! It's like these people expect to eat a full meal and then jump on the Peloton right away. If I eat a meal and don't feel tired afterward, that wasn't a successful meal.

"So," I said to Katie. "You don't eat gluten?"

"I know, it sucks. I love gluten. But I have . . . celiac disease."

Looks like I was keeping those ten dates after all.

---

*In my opinion, paleo is the most asinine of all the food trends. The rule is, eat like cavemen used to eat. Cool. Let's get our health advice from people who lived to the ripe old age of twenty.

Celiac disease afflicts 1 percent of the world's population, and somehow, someway, all those people live in L.A. You can imagine my skepticism. Celiac disease lets people out here justify not eating carbs. I've seen this game before: like my mother's "allergy" to shellfish. Not only that, you can bet that 99 percent of the 1 percent of the world that has celiac disease are beautiful, white, blond, skinny, and living in L.A. Katie checked all the boxes.

Celiac seems to be the only disease people are proud to have. People in L.A. love talking about having this disease. Anywhere. Parties ("Thank *God* they have gluten-free cupcakes. I have *such* a sweet tooth, and a sweet disease. Celiac disease!"). Funerals ("Such a shame about Mary. She left us too soon. But hey, at least she lived a full life, full of gluten. Something I can never have, because I have celiac disease."). At the Apple Store ("Hi, do you guys have the new iPhone 14? No? All good. At least I still have celiac disease."). Celiackers have no humility about their ailment. No other disease elicits such pride. You never hear people say, "Guys. Guys. You're not going to believe this. I just got off the phone with my doctor. I have not one, not two, but *multiple* sclerosis!"

Before Katie mentioned celiac, I was nervous as hell to talk to her. Once she was no longer a potential mate, I could relax and ease into the conversation. Taking my nerves down a notch let her lower her wall, and suddenly the room around us faded as we clicked. Even if Jim Carrey screamed "ALRIGHTY THEN!" it would've gone over our heads. I dug her. She seemed to dig me. But when I know there's absolutely no food relationship happening with the person, I no longer relate to them in a sexual way. I might have been talking to a good buddy. A buddy who happened to be the most beautiful woman I had ever spoken to in my life. She was interested in developing a show for TV, but didn't know how. I told her about selling a show about Falafel Phil. She had never heard of him, and the story blew her away.

Before leaving, I gave her my number and said if she needed help, she could call me. Mind you, this was two years after my broken engagement to Isabelle, when I was desperate to meet a good partner. Yet, when I'm finally ready to get out there, and I meet an amazing woman, she does *nothing* for me, because celiac. Not only that, Katie invited me to her upcoming birthday party, and I told her I couldn't make it because I was going on a date. That's the level of chutzpah this nerd had, talking to an enchantress.

A few days later I was enjoying one of my epic food walks: I take an Uber to downtown Los Angeles, and walk back the twenty-three miles to my house, through Koreatown. I stop at random hole-in-the-wall bars and restaurants and stores on the way. I have some repeat stops. Five miles in lies the Korean supermarket called Hannam. I'm enamored with Korean supermarkets in L.A. Where I'm from, the ethnic markets are tiny shacks with two aisles of hyper-packed immigrant ingredients chucked up on shelves with no regard to alphabetical order or product placement. A knocked-over bottle of pomegranate molasses can lie awkwardly next to a lone bag of dried kidney beans that sits atop Swiffer wet pad refills—all in an aisle labeled "Ramadan Stuffs."

The Korean supermarkets in L.A. are what every other immigrant market strives to be—the same size as a huge supermarket, except everything in there is Korean, and clean, and organized, and beautiful. Also, their sample game is *on point.* While at your local supermarket you'll maybe get samples of some crappy cheddar cheese or the newest energy bar, a Korean supermarket offers fifteen to twenty amazingly fun samples at a time: fiery soups with braised pork neck, kimchi fried rice, and my favorite Korean snack ever, ojingeochae. Think squid candy. Squid is dehydrated, then seasoned with sugar and gochujang, a Korean fermented chili paste. It's sweet, spicy, stringy, chewy, tangy, the best! As the poor lady doling out samples gave me the stink eye, knowing I wasn't buying anything, Katie texted me.

"How was your date, Dan the man?"

"Still single," I wrote back. We texted back and forth as I made my way to my next stop at mile thirteen—Feng Mao BBQ.

Tiny Feng Mao specializes in Korean-style grilled lamb. I wish I could tell you how they make it, but I have no idea. Whenever I ask them, they do the immigrant move my parents do—they pretend not to speak English when it's convenient.

"Hi, welcome to Feng Mao. Can I start you off with an appetizer or beverage?"

"Sure, I'll take a beer, and five lamb skewers."

"Beer and skewers, you got it."

"Thanks. Also, that special marinade on the lamb—what is it exactly?"

"Sorry . . . no . . . English."

I don't blame them for keeping a secret, because they have

the holy grail of marinades. I wouldn't be surprised if the main ingredient was the tears of the members of BTS.* What I can tell you is that it's absolutely the best bite of food you can find in Los Angeles. Five mini kebab skewers arrive raw at your table. You're given a white Mickey Mouse glove to help with the heat, and you grill the marinated kebabs tableside. The skewers of lamb hold a bright red oil slick of gooey goodness clinging to the flesh. Once on the grill, the red caramelizes into a deep crimson with a few charred black areas, where the flames got a lick in. After the skewers are removed from the grill, you fork the cubes of lamb, which sizzle as they slide off. The cubes are small, about the size of a die, but when you squish one between your molars, an explosion of savory overwhelms your mouth. I wish I could tell you the flavors at work, but sorry . . . no . . . English.

I love going to Feng Mao by myself because marinating in this otherworldly flavor alone—being able to savor every bite, sometimes eyes shut, looking ridiculous—brings me joy. But this day, I wasn't savoring, I wasn't giving much thought to the lamb. My attention was caught by the text chain going back and forth between me and Katie. She was funny, and quick. And though I knew we weren't going to work out, I perked up every time I was graced with a response. So transfixed was I by Katie that I blindly flexed my chopsticks into the rice bowl, not realizing I had finished the lamb.

I paid the bill and kept walking, texting all the while. The

---

*Although it's probably MSG. Oh, also, BTS is a Korean boy band—one of the most successful boy bands in history, as it so happens. And why shouldn't they be! With iconic lyrics like "Stop playing hard to get before I kick you in the butt," or the classic "You were even born with sexy brain wrinkles." Yup. All real.

fun thing about walking around in Los Angeles is that you see places you just pass by in your car. At mile nineteen I saw a solitary red light next to a tiny red canopy in front of a nondescript store in a strip mall. The letters above the canopy read DA SARANG KARAOKE & BAR. Why the fuck not?

Most karaoke bars in Los Angeles are big labyrinths with private rooms for drunk white people to wile out* in. This was not that. It was a tiny watering hole, red lighting everywhere, and a mean, skinny old lady behind the bar held a mini megaphone in her hand to announce the next singer. On some tight couches sat small groups of well-dressed men who drank soju with women who were clearly not their wives. One depressed red-faced blue-collar man slumped at the end of the bar, wailing into the microphone a sad off-key Korean song that seemed to be his substitute for therapy. In this dingy den people came to hide, blow off steam, and do unsavory things.

I took a seat at the bar, pissing off the old lady, who hoped I'd leave of my own accord. She wielded the mini megaphone like a bludgeon.

"Hi."

Nothing.

"Can I order, please?"

Nothing.

"I'll take a Hite beer and some tteokbokki."

Her eyes suddenly opened, and her scowl turned into a smile.

"How do you know tteokbokki?"

"I *love* tteokbokki!"

*"Wile out" means "go crazy," Mom.

She opened a beer, set it before me, and went to the kitchen to make my dish. She was not only the karaoke MC, she was also, astonishingly, the chef.

Tteokbokki is probably the most popular Korean bar food, and it pairs better with beer than anything you can get in an Oktoberfest tent. Gummy four-inch cylinders of pulverized rice are served in a funky, kelpy, spicy red fishy broth. It's grimy, perfect for this setting. I basked in my favorite immersive experience—awesome food and drink, weird–people watching, acceptance in a place where I don't belong. I live for moments like this. But I found myself shunning all these pleasures for my phone. And before I knew it, I texted:

"Hey what are you doing tomorrow?"

"No plans."

"Let's grab a drink . . ."

"Sounds good!"

I walked the final mile home smiling, yet rationalizing, "This isn't a date. This girl might just be a cool friend." Dan Ahdoot didn't date girls with food restrictions.

Then I met her the next night.

I sat waiting for her at the Tower Bar at the iconic Sunset Tower Hotel. Classy, Old Hollywood. Mahogany wood, a crackling fireplace, leather seats, Art Deco lamps, Count Basie in the background, silver cocktail shakers shaking in the fore—a far distance in every way from my karaoke bar of the previous evening. I ordered a Negroni and made small talk with the bartender until Katie entered. This bar draws beautiful people, but once she arrived, everyone else looked pedestrian. She wore a sophisticated black dress that hugged her body. This outfit demanded fancy heels, but she wore rad distressed designer sneakers instead. Her blond locks, no longer tied in a bun, cascaded down her shoulders in elegant lush layers. In jet-black eyeliner that contrasted sharply with her light Nordic features, she looked like a movie star from the sixties, missing only the long white gloves and Bakelite cigarette holder. She was a gluten-free goddess.

After a barrage of fun banter, a few hours and rounds later, we talked about our last relationships. Talking about a past love affair with a potential new mate is always weird. You feel you have to spin the tale so you look good, or sympathetic, or noble. Like answering that dumb job interview question "What's your biggest weakness?" "My biggest weakness is that I'm not happy at home if I don't know my boss is having the best day of his life." I guess the relationship version of that answer would be "We broke up because I gave as much as I could and it still wasn't enough." You know, that bullshit.

Well, since I didn't see Katie as a potential mate, I could be brutally honest. I told her everything that went right. Everything that went wrong. My faults. My ex's faults. All was out on the table. Katie had a tenderness and loving way of speaking to my failed relationship that I hadn't found from friends, family, or therapists after my breakup. She was perfect . . . just not for me.

Our tenure at the bar was reaching its natural close, but we both didn't want the night to end.

"Hey, do you want to do something crazy?" I asked.

"Uh-oh. Is this where you recruit me to Scientology?"

We chuckled as I ordered an Uber.

"It's a surprise. And it's Xenu approved."

At the karaoke joint the night before, I'd been wearing gross gym shorts and a ripped T-shirt; my hair was sweaty and unkempt; there was stubble on my face. Now dressed to the nines, cleanly shaven, with a female deity on my arm, I presented a different story. The old lady scowled, not recognizing me.

"Remember me? From yesterday?" Still nothing. "Tteokbokki?"

She lit up again. "You were ugly yesterday!"

Katie and I laughed and sat at the bar. This epitome of elegance, in this dank smoke-filled room, was a sight to see. She played it cool. The sticky bar, the Korean gangsters, the depressed singers, they were all there, yet she made no fuss, didn't look at her watch—she went straight for the huge, laminated binder, took the slip of paper, the mini pencil, and wrote in her song, as if this were her regular joint.

"What are you singing?" I asked.

"It's a surprise," she said.

Once this night's slumped-over crooner finished his depressing Korean ballad, something I imagine was entitled "Why the Fuck Am I Still Living," the old lady called, "Katie. You sing."

"That's me!" she said, and grabbed the mic. I was imagining she would sing a typical crowd-pleaser—Elton John, Fleetwood Mac, Coldplay.

She sang Eminem. And not just any Eminem—she sang "Stan." It's basically Eminem angrily reading out a fan's string of letters that start off benignly and end up descending into madness. Katie knew every word, and everyone stared at the camera-ready movie star rapping like a lunatic. It was magical. When she finished, the whole bar of misfits went nuts. They had never seen anything like it before. I had never seen anything like it before. I had found the perfect woman.

Then the tteokbokki hit the bar.

The old woman had brought us a gift. "Tteokbokki!" She stared at us both, eagerly awaiting our first bites.

Katie, who just a minute before had the bar dizzy under her spell, looked at me sheepishly, then at the old lady, then back at me.

"Do you think there's gluten in this?" she whispered.

"No, it's rice."

"But what about soy sauce?"

"You can't have soy sauce?"

"It's made with wheat."

"You can't eat it?" said the old lady.

Another depressed Korean started to sing a song called "Please Kill Me Now."

"You can't have soy sauce?" I said, in disbelief.

"No, I can't," she said, embarrassed.

"Eat, eat!" said the lady.

"I'm pretty sure there's soy sauce in this," I said.

"Then I can't have it."

"Really? Even a little?"

"Will you excuse me for a minute?" She went to the bathroom.

As I started to eat the tteokbokki, my fantasy shattered. Here we were being gifted food—to me the highest expression of praise—and we couldn't share it. Sharing a meal is my way of connecting with the world, and not to be able to do that with a partner is devastating.

When Katie returned from the bathroom, I ate way too much food, trying to compensate for her not having any.

"I'm sorry—"

"No, it's totally fine. More for me."

I took her back to her place. She lived in a luxury high-rise apartment with good lighting, expensive scented candles, music, and art. We had a glass of champagne on her balcony and kissed under a sliver of the moon. She was the most beautiful, accomplished, funny, caring, and charming woman I had ever kissed in my life. And even enjoying this fairy tale, all I could think about was how we couldn't be together. My whole raison d'être had become restaurants, and amending that focus even a little bit felt like such an affront to my identity that I couldn't let go fully in the moment.

For a few days I didn't reach out, but the more time I spent away from her, the more she filled my mind. I remember speaking to Mo about her, giving the download, and ending, "I don't think I'll see her again."

Mo fed my words back to me with a surgeon's precision. "So, you're saying you met the hottest girl you've ever met; she's cool, funny, and awesome. The conversation was great. And you don't want to go out with her again."

"Yeah, but the gluten allergy."

"Right. Don't be fucking stupid, Dan. I gotta run."

Katie and I started dating. I had never been so floored by love in my life. When we were together, any insecurity I had faded to the recesses of my mind. This is a big deal, because I have a lot of them. But being with Katie was cleansing. I felt more like myself when I was with her, because she accepted me 150 percent. She was proud of me, she respected me, and she loved me with an authenticity I'd never known possible. She was flawless . . . except when we went to restaurants.

Katie was so afraid of mistakenly ingesting gluten that every time we ate out, she conducted an intense interrogation of the server. Every dish had to be verbally broken down into its base parts. Substitutions were requested often, and the chef-driven haunts I loved were not so accommodating. Restaurants, my happy places, where I could let myself go into the hands of a culinary artist, suddenly became dens of potential poisoning. As much as I loved her, I couldn't live this way. So, I broke up with her, smack-dab in the middle of our honeymoon phase. She didn't understand why I made my choice, but she respected it. She wasn't going to push to be with someone who didn't want to be with her. She was better than that.

Months went by, and I missed Katie immensely. Every day I wasn't with her lay heavily on me, because the more time went by, the more my asinine food brain atrophied and all that was left was her void. I went out on other dates, with people who ate freely, but I felt not an ounce of the connection I felt with Katie.

I started to think maybe I was missing out on a huge opportunity. A chance at redemption. My past relationship with Isabelle should not have lasted more than a few months, but our food bond led me to propose marriage. I no longer wanted to be led by food. It had brought me to a lot of great places but also many wrong ones. I wasn't going to let things I ate fuck up my life again.

I reached out to Katie and convinced her to get back together with me. She was apprehensive, as she should've been, but I assured her that I was clear on what mattered, and that being with her was more important than any joy food could bring me.

Things were great. I didn't focus on food; I focused on Katie. We stayed in and ordered takeout most nights, which helped. Other nights I cooked. I tried to avoid restaurants, knowing they were my main triggers, which left me free to open my heart to Katie. I even unfollowed eateries on Instagram so I wasn't as tempted to go out. And yes, I know this sounds childish, but I figured if I could concentrate on her and not the restaurants, it would fill me with so much love that eventually the restaurants wouldn't need to mean so much.

It didn't work. As soon as we ate out, the voice in my head would awaken from its slumber. "C'mon, Dan. Really? You're going to be with someone who has dietary restrictions? This isn't you." I told Katie about the voice. And that's what I thought it was: this inner voice, distinct from what I wanted, motivated only by food, that was sabotaging my relationship.

To Katie's credit, to show you the kind of person she is, she never gave me any grief for the voice. She never judged it or made me feel stupid. Just the opposite, she did what she could to accommodate it. When she ordered takeout, she would leave the room so I didn't have to hear the breakdown of ingredients with the person on the other end. The voice was kept at bay, for a while.

Then I tried to enact workarounds myself so I could avoid the back-and-forth with the server. I'd tell Katie what I wanted, then head to the bathroom, hoping the interrogation would be over before I returned. This practice was unsustainable.

I went to therapy to shut the voice down, and that didn't work. Slowly, I chipped away at Katie's comfort. I replaced the hardwood floors in every restaurant with a surface of eggshells, and there was no way she wasn't going to break a couple. She began to get nervous around me, more reserved. I in turn would get angry that she wasn't being herself. The tension between us reached a fever pitch when the voice in my head, ever so resourceful, started playing a new tune.

I had heard about Katie's celiac "episodes" when she mistakenly ate gluten. She would vomit nonstop for a full day. At this point we had been together just over a year, and I had yet to observe an episode. Was it possible she hadn't mistakenly ingested a shred of wheat in all that time? I started to probe her about her episodes, and the voice concluded, "Baby, I don't think you have celiac disease. I think you had food poisoning and confused it with celiac disease." Katie looked at me doubtfully. The voice was getting louder.

But I wanted what was best for her! Even if it was best for me. What if I was right? What if it *was* food poisoning? Wouldn't that benefit her? To be free from the burden of constantly thinking she was on the verge of being poisoned wherever she went? Although she responded with numbness, I took initiative. She just needed to be helped, and I was the guy to do it. I found a gastroenterologist in Los Angeles who specialized in celiac disease. All she had to do was go for some tests, and when we found out she was fine, I would marry her in a heartbeat.

At this time Katie was the lead on a TV show, and her face rose high on billboards. She was on top of the world, and I was doing everything in my power to shine a light on her imperfections. If only she could help me kill the voice.

The tests came back. She had celiac disease.

I even doubted the result.

She couldn't take it anymore. And in her moment of despair in front of me, through tears and agony, she realized I wasn't going to change, and that this misery would go on forever. Rather than let her go, I assured her I would try my best to put an end to this, to exorcise the voice. And she stood by me. She was the one who needed the love, and still I took and took.

One day we went to République, a swanky French restaurant in West Hollywood. We sat at the bar and ordered champagne and oysters. Katie mustered up the "There's no gluten in this, right?" The bartender responded rudely, "Is there . . . gluten . . . in oysters? No. There's no gluten." He walked away, leaving the sound of a thousand eggshells cracking.

"Was that necessary?" I scolded. "Gluten in the fucking oysters?"

"Dan, I'm sorry, but I don't know if maybe there's something in the mignonette."

"I need a minute," I said, and walked out of the restaurant. A few minutes later I walked back in, and we ate in silence. The most unpleasant champagne and oysters ever consumed.

Shortly after this we broke up. Again. The initial relief was elating. My triumph starved the voice of oxygen, and I could breathe easy. Weeks went by. And again, slowly, the voice on mute, I started to miss her. I didn't want to get back together, but I wanted to know she still cared about me. I would post a story on Instagram and check every minute to see if she had seen it. That kind of childish thing. But missing anyone after a breakup is natural, so I decided to give it time.

Time did nothing, and a few months later I admitted to Mo that I wasn't getting any better. Mo did what Mo always does. He suggested a hunting trip. "Bro, you need to get your mind off this. Let's go into the woods. I just drew a tag for Coues deer in Arizona. Just me and you, camping, hunting, eating great food, and drinking great wine." It was a compelling offer, and I needed a change. So I went.

Coues deer are the hardest deer to hunt in North America. They live in extremely rugged territory, in the mountains of Arizona. It's a jagged, dusty, violent landscape. The deer live in an area full of natural predators, so they have evolved to elude them. They have become masters at hiding. They're tiny, among the smallest deer in the world, about half the size of a typical whitetail, more like a Doberman pinscher. They are the color of their surroundings and live amid immense amounts of brush. They don't move a ton, to preserve energy in the desert's extreme heat. Here's how you hunt them: You hike up a mountain that's opposite another mountain. Then you find a good vantage point, sit down, take out binoculars, and scan the mountain all the way from one side to the other, slowly looking for the deer (it's called glassing). Once you find the deer, you stalk them.

At this point in my life, I was no longer a beginner. While Mo was clearly the better hunter, I didn't need any hand-holding. Plus, I wasn't hunting at all on this trip. I didn't draw a tag, so the pressure of getting an animal was all on Mo's shoulders. I could sit back, relax, and relish the show. Enjoying the outdoors with a buddy, clearing my head. We met at the Phoenix airport, and I hugged him hard.

"Dude, I needed this," I said.

"Me too, bro. Let's get my gun."

We headed to the Special Services area of the airport, where stern-faced hunters and buttoned-up golfers stand together waiting for their gear. We got the rifle and headed out. Mo is a great listener, and on the three-hour drive to our campsite, I unloaded my last few months. Telling him what happened gave me the therapy session I needed. I put my music on, and he was like "Dude, put my playlist on."

"Okay, let's just listen to some of my stuff first."

"No, dude, seriously, my playlist is awesome."

"Okay, you got it." I put on his music, and we kept driving.

We got to the campsite as the sun was going down, and I took in our home for the week. The air was brisk, cusping on cold. It smelled of dry pine—like how a chilled sauna would smell. It was gorgeous. Not a car in sight. The pale moon sat in its place, waiting for the lights to go out so it could show off its curves. I took a few deep breaths.

"This is awesome," I said.

"Yeah, let's unload before it gets dark."

"Okay, in a minute, let me just take this in."

"You can take it in once we have our gear out. C'mon, let's go."

I started to unload the truck. We put up our tent pretty quickly, got a fire started,* and I began to cook some steaks while we drank good red wine. I took a big sip. This was living.

---

*I did *not* bring any cigars.

Mo took out his Garmin GPS and thrust the bright screen in my face. "Okay, so for tomorrow, I think we should start here, then go to this spot here, and glass in the morning as the sun comes up."

"Okay," I said. "Can we just enjoy our meal and then talk business?"

"I mean, yeah, we can, but we should probably go over this, so we don't have to look at it later."

"Yeah, okay, whatever."

He droned on about coordinates as I blocked him out and tried to savor hanger steak and mushrooms.

Mo smacked my leg. "Aight, bro, let's do a gear check."

He got up to head toward the tent.

"Mo," I said, "I'm still eating."

"It's getting late, and we have to be up before the sun."

"I know, can I just finish my fucking dinner?"

"Okay, bro, relax."

"Yeah, that's what I'm trying to do."

He went into the tent to check his gear as I finished my dinner. I was annoyed. Moreover, I was annoyed that I was annoyed. This trip was supposed to clear my mind with a buddy, and suddenly I felt like a child on a trip with his dad. I finished my steak, headed to the tent, and joined him in my gear check.

"Did you bring hand warmers?"

"Yup."

"Did you download the local maps?"

"Yup."

"Did you buy those boots I told you to buy?"

"No, dude, I told you, my boots are fine."

"You didn't buy them?"

"No, I didn't buy them."

"But I told you to buy them, bro."

"Mo, I'm not going to spend four hundred dollars on new boots when mine are fine. Also, is this a gear check or an interrogation?"

My pitch rose with my frustration.

"Okay, fine. What layers are you wearing tomorrow? It gets cold."

I couldn't take it anymore.

"Mo, you need to chill the fuck out. Stop talking to me like I'm one of your surgical nurses."

"Dude, relax, I'm just making sure you're good."

"I'm good. I can dress myself. You do you."

We finished the rest of our gear setup in silence. Eventually we got into bed and turned the lights out. I had a little too much adrenaline coursing through me to sleep easily. Mo cut the quiet.

"Hey, I'm sorry. I can be like that sometimes. I guess it's just being an older brother and a surgeon, I'm very used to doling out orders."

It was soothing to hear. "Thanks, man, I appreciate it."

We went to bed, the crackle of our fire as our white noise.

We were up at four o'clock to the dulcet tones of our iPhone alarms. I made some instant coffee and started suiting up, excited to explore new topography and be immersed in nature. We began to hike out of camp, into the wild, in full darkness, using our headlamps to guide us.

The topography was brutal. This area seemed less like a mountain and more like a rescue for jagged rocks—as if helicopters and bulldozers had spent eons haphazardly dumping the most annoying rocks on top of one another to create these very mountains. You couldn't look up and walk. Our eyes were planted on our feet as we tried to stay on whatever best resembled solid ground. If we looked up for a second, we could slip, our arms spread comically wide and useless. The random scattering of rattlesnakes also reinforced that looking down was the way to go.

Add to that the pissed-off flora—everything thorny and bone-dry. If you grazed any of the plants, they'd make sure you knew it. They were out for blood. We also had to step over a bunch of barbed wire. The federal government lets farmers graze their livestock on public lands for a fee. It's good for the farmers because it's cheap food and exercise for their animals. It's good for the forests because livestock grazing increases plant diversity, regenerates native habitats, and reduces wildfire threats. However, it's really shitty for me and Mo because every half a mile or so, we had to climb over a hip-high, rusty barbed wire fence while carrying all of our gear. One of us would find a place on the wire without barbs, wrap our hand around it, and press the fence down as the other sidled over it, occasionally ripping pants and skin. I came on this trip to clear my head of my breakup, not to struggle through Tetanus Mountain in the dark.

We hiked up a few miles, exhausted by the altitude, focused, eyes fixed down, racing before the sun rose to get to a good vantage point and start glassing. We found a clear piece of ground, sat down, pulled out our binoculars, and waited. It was quiet. The wind was slow to wake up, gently making its presence felt, as if it were hungover from a raucous night of howling. The sun rose from behind us and started to stir the mountain we were set to glass. Mo and I were panting as our breath was literally and figuratively taken away.

Initially, we were treated to a silhouette of the mountain. Then the clouds above it, frothy cappuccino foam, came into view. The flora joined in next, dense and fluid from a distance. Every second this beast of a mountain got brighter and brighter, showing off more of its majesty. A cliff here, a ravine there. There's nothing like the slow reveal of nature at first light. I remember thinking how the mountain we were staring at was, for all intents and purposes, the same as the mountain we were sitting on. However, from close up it was an awful hellscape, and from a distance it was the epitome of beauty.

When it was light enough, we took out our monopods, set our binoculars on top, and started to glass. Left to right, then down a notch, then right to left. Your eyes dart slowly, much like the snake on the Nokia phone game from back in the day.* And it starts out really fun—like *Where's Waldo?* in real life. We were both super eager to find a Coues deer and start stalking.

An hour went by, no deer. Two hours, no deer.

"This is tough," I said to Mo.

"Yeah, I thought for sure we'd see one by now."

"Maybe we're too far away?"

"Shhh."

Shhh? We were hunting for an animal three miles away on another mountain. Why was he telling me to shhh?

I stayed quiet. Then ten minutes later, Mo whispered, "We should probably get closer."

---

*I am fully aware that only 1 percent of you will get this reference, but it's worth it for you guys. Enjoy.

"Oh, weird, because I suggested that ten minutes ago, and you told me to shhh."

He packed up and started walking. I stayed back a little, staring at him, irate. I picked up my binoculars and followed.

We got closer and started glassing again. One hour of going back and forth over the same land and seeing absolutely nothing. It *was* like playing *Where's Waldo?* but here's the catch—there was no fucking Waldo.

We saw nothing on the first day. We saw nothing on the second.

What I did see, though, was the effect Mo was having on me. He was controlling my every move. The way I packed in the morning—"Bring your vest out, it's going to be cold." My thoughts on the hunt—"Nah, we shouldn't go that route, let's go my way." Even the way I walked. "Make sure you step a little softer, and don't cough so loud."

"Oh, so if I inhale dust, I should just slowly choke to death. Got it."

"Stop being a dick."

"Me? You're literally telling me not to cough."

"Well, I don't want you to scare away an animal and ruin my hunt!"

There it was. This was not me and Mo going out into the woods together to bond. No, I was his sherpa on his hunt, and in his mind, that gave him the right to run the show. Had I known my role, I would have stayed home.

Every hour that went by, I became more and more quiet. I initially voiced my dislike of the way Mo talked to me, but after seeing that my words had no effect, I decided to minimize myself. I knew hearing him talk to me like that was going to anger me, so I decided to remove as much stimuli as I could. I stopped making suggestions and replaced all original thought with "whatever you think, dude." In a way, I became like the deer we were hunting. Their response to threats was to minimize themselves. I was doing the same thing.

On the third day, we reached our spot and started to glass. By now I hated this hunt and couldn't wait for it to end. I focused as hard as I could so we could find a deer, kill it, and get the fuck off this mountain. Scowling through binoculars at nature, I grew so frustrated, the hairs on the back on my neck stood up at attention. All I wanted to do was scream at the top of my lungs and chuck my binoculars into the air, when Mo finally said, "Holy fucking shit."

"What?"

"I got one."

"No fucking way."

"Dude, this is insane."

He guided me through my binoculars, getting me to the deer using the landmarks that had been made familiar to us over the past three days.

"Okay, you see the Afro tree? Go down halfway between there and Peter's nose.* Now go to the left; there're three trees. In between the first and second one."

"I'm there. I don't see anything."

"Wait a second. He'll move."

When the deer moved, it wasn't at all what I had imagined. He was so well camouflaged that it looked more like the earth had shifted a bit than that an animal had moved.

---

*A jumbled pile of rocks that looked like our college buddy's nose.

"Holy shit. How did you see that?"

"I don't know. I just happened to be there and saw something move."

We both looked up from our binoculars to each other.

"This is wild!"

"It's crazy."

We looked back into the binoculars.

"Oh no."

"No no no no! Shit!"

He was gone. It's immensely difficult to keep eyes on these animals. Now that we knew the minute level of observation we needed to use, deer started popping up more and more.

Eventually we locked eyes on a nice buck feeding near a dried riverbed. He grazed in a rare patch of land that didn't have much cover, so he couldn't disappear so easily.

"What do you think?" said Mo.

I couldn't believe he was asking my opinion. And I hated how happy that made me.

"Let's cross the barbed wire to the left of us, go down into the valley, and then climb up on the other side."

"Okay."

"Cool."

"But if we go down straight, we can cut him off in case he decides to head west."

"Okay, but if he doesn't head west, we might spook him. The wind is headed in his direction."

"Yeah."

Silence.

"Let's go straight down," he said, and he started to pack his gear.

I was numb at this point. I felt like I meant nothing on this trip. Why the fuck was I even here? My opinion meant nothing; my presence was insignificant.

We made it down the mountain and started our ascent up the other side. The riverbed was just ahead of us.

"I think you should chamber a round," I whispered.

"Shhh."

I was done. If Mo were to train his binoculars on me, I wouldn't be there. In fact, as we ascended one slow step at a time, trying to disturb the least amount of rock underfoot, I was rooting for the Coues deer way more than for Mo.

I looked down for a second, looked back up, and there he was. In a quick cut from a horror film, a tiny full-size buck stood thirty yards in front of us. My heart skipped a beat. I turned around and Mo was on his phone, checking out the GPS map.

"MO!" I pointed frantically at the deer. Mo dropped the phone and put his gun to his shoulder. He had a clear shot and took it. However, there was no bullet in the chamber. "Fuck!" He put the gun down and quickly racked. The deer was gone before Mo got his gun back up.

"I told you to chamber your gun!" I said at full volume. "Why don't you listen to a word I fucking say?!"

"Shut up! He might still be here!"

"Fuck you," I said and started walking back to camp with zero regard to hiding my presence. Honestly, I wanted the deer to hear me so Mo would have no chance. Each step I took away from him slowly undid his grip on my psyche until I was alone in the woods, free to get what I came for. A solitary moment with nature to clear my head.

But it didn't clear. A dam broke and it flooded.

It's not that Mo was the predator, and I was the Coues deer. No, I was the predator, and Katie was the Coues. Rather than allow her to be, I forced my will on her and made her succumb to my rules. Rules that I created to lash out against my parents' coping mechanism for losing their son. My brother dies, they find comfort in religion, and rather than let them be, I judge the new shred of meaning they eke out from the catastrophe of watching their twenty-year-old wither away in front of their eyes. And I committed to my rules so hard that I became a gluten tyrant to the only person who loved me unconditionally.

Did I *really* love food that much? Enough to choose it over the greatest woman to ever enter my life? What if my food voice was doubt? Doubt? But I never had doubts when it came to big things. I didn't have doubt when I decided to become a comedian against my parents' wishes—trading in the cushy life of a doctor for that of a broke beginner comic with zero stability. I had zero doubt that I was going to succeed—in the face of friends, family, and statistics telling me otherwise.

The difference was that I was committed to being a comedian. And I never committed to Katie. I never took the relationship as seriously as I needed to because I was Dan Ahdoot and I could never take a relationship seriously if food wasn't front and center. What a joke. I thought food was the only thing that made me interesting. I found a person who didn't care about my food bona fides. She loved me for me. And I pushed her away because of vanity.

Committing to my career made all doubt disappear. Commitment to Katie was going to do the same.

When Mo got back to camp, I apologized for my outburst.

The trip ended up being a godsend. I came for peace of mind, but Mo gave me exactly what I needed—a taste of my own medicine.[*]

I got back to Los Angeles and called my mother to overnight an heirloom family wedding ring. I remember thinking on a Monday how crazy it was that I was going to be engaged by the weekend.

I called Katie. It went to voicemail.

"Hey, it's Dan. Sorry this is out of nowhere, but please call me. I need to talk to you."

No reply for a day. So I sent a text. "Hey! Do you think we can talk?"

No reply.

I weighed just driving over to her place with the ring but wanted to be respectful of boundaries. I had ruined the relationship by taking control. I wanted her to be in control of opening the door to me.

I started assembling care packages for her, full of personal items I knew she loved, and heartfelt letters.

Three days, three care packages, three letters.

Finally, I got a text.

"Hi. Please stop sending the packages. I'm not in a place to talk right now."

I showed this text to some friends, and they were crestfallen. "I'm so sorry, Dan." Their reaction confused me. "She wrote 'right now.' That means eventually there will be a chance! I just have to wait."

---

[*]Mo, don't take this to mean you can always treat me like shit because a lesson sits on the other side. Once is plenty.

I waited, each day thinking it would be the day she would make contact. Weeks went by. Weeks turned to months. I did nothing but think of her in hopes that we could finally be together. I couldn't eat. I couldn't sleep. I was confident she would appear, but no amount of glassing seemed to bring her into view. She had become as elusive as the Coues deer. I made her that way.

Katie never responded to me, and eventually I found out she was dating somebody. I tried to dig up any details about the guy, but all I could get was, "He treats her really, really nicely." I could see that as being a balm to the way I treated her.

What would've happened if Katie had given me another chance? Would the commitment have really changed things? Would the voice still have come back after some time? I don't think so, but who knows. What if my food voice is not a separate entity after all? Maybe it's my most authentic self. Maybe I was turning myself into a Coues deer. Minimizing myself in the hope of winning her back.

I don't know. What I do know is that, ironically, the moments I dreaded sharing with Katie are now the ones when I can't stop thinking about her: when I go to restaurants. Especially when I hear someone pleading with the server for gluten-free substitutions. It used to make me cringe. Now it fills me with melancholy. I would give anything to hear Katie ask if there's gluten in the oysters.

10

FORGETTING
IN PARIS

MY FATHER LOVES THE EXPRESSION "YOU CAN BE SAD ON A BUS, OR you can be sad in a Rolls-Royce. But it's a little nicer to be sad in a Rolls-Royce."

My breakup with Katie inspired me to get into a Rolls-Royce. I was developing a TV show and because I could write from anywhere, I rented an Airbnb in Saint-Germain-des-Prés in Paris. I had never been to Paris and was excited to embark on a gluttonous culinary adventure to eat, drink, and most probably get gout. I did extensive research, called in some favors, and made a bunch of ridiculous reservations. I couldn't wait to get out of Los Angeles, where every corner reminded me of my ex and every meal held a bad memory. And also, there was a girl.

Years before, I was in New York City with my buddy Mike. We were having a bite at a cute little French restaurant in No-lita called Cafe Gitane when, suddenly, an astonishing woman walked through the door. She was wearing tight jeans, ballet flats, and a slightly oversize white button-down. She had slick black hair that followed her jawline, giving a fierce angle to what was a breathtaking visage. Her skin was smooth, olive colored, her eyes a light almond. She was fit, in that European way; her petite, elegant physique came not from SoulCycle and fad diets, but from cigarettes and decadence in moderation—unstudied, unmade-up, natural beauty. She sat down a few tables away from us.

Mike noticed too. "Wow."

"Right?"

That was all that needed to be said. We went back to our conversation, but my eyes kept checking in. I was fascinated. She kept looking at her watch and at the door. Who was she? Who was she waiting for?

"I have to do something," I said to Mike.

I scribbled on a little napkin and called over our server. "Hey," I asked. "Would you mind giving this napkin to that woman along with a glass of champagne?"

She was game. "Absolutely."

Mike and I watched with eager excitement as the champagne landed with the note. I was shivering with nerves. The server whispered in her ear, then she looked over at me. I did my worst slick hand gesture—it looked more like I was playing Rock Paper Scissors and just threw Scissors in her direction.

Still she smiled and read the note:

"Waiting is more fun with champagne. —Dan and Mike"

Her smile grew. Her two front teeth were angled slightly away from one another. An embodiment of adorable I never knew I needed. She got up and started walking toward us.

"Holy shit," I said to Mike.

She strolled over and bent at the knees right next to me, nonchalantly pulling her hair away out of her eyes, leaving her face just inches from mine. The hairs on my arm stood up.

"Um, yeah, we saw you're waiting and thought maybe some champagne would be nice. Do you like champagne?" I bumbled.

And she said sheepishly, in a French accent that glided out of her mouth like cigarette smoke during a passive exhale:

"I'm so sorry. My English is . . . uh . . . pas très bien."

I was exultant.

"Moi je parle français!"

As I mentioned before, my father had raised me speaking French, and for all I knew, the whole purpose of that instruction was to train me for this moment right here.

Cafe Gitane is tiny and she seemed uncomfortable in her crouch. So I moved my chair over a bit. "S'il te plâit. Joins toi à nous."

Suddenly she was snuggled against me. She smelled of modern unisex perfume that skewed masculine—iris and leather. She explained she was meeting a friend and returning to Paris the next day.

"If you ever come to Paris, I will buy you a glass of champagne."

"That's a deal. Oh. Je m'appelle Dan. Et toi?"

"Carole.* Enchantée."

When I decided, three years later, to take a trip to Paris, I decided to cash in my champagne check with Carole.

Heart still badly bruised after my breakup with Katie, I wasn't in a place to be romantically involved with anyone. But I figured all bets are off when you're in Paris.

I sat outside a seafood-focused bistro called Huguette— a place of her choosing. Scanning my watch, then the street, I searched for someone resembling the Carole from our first encounter. In New York, she seemed lost, a little out of place. Nervous from her lack of the vernacular. But now when I saw her walking toward me, I recognized right away we were on her home turf. A cashmere camel-colored overcoat, black leather pants, red Jordan high-tops, smoking a cigarette. She owned the cobblestones she stepped on.

She came over, we kissed a bunch of times on the cheek, and she sat down next to me. All the chairs in the cafés were next to one another, facing out, an unwritten rule that the people in this city are meant to be watched.

"I can't believe you're here," she said.

"I know. Me neither!"†

"Did you order anything?"

"No, I'm waiting for the champagne you owe me."

The first things I ate in Paris were French oysters from Brittany—which aren't as briny and funky as East Coast oysters, or as dainty and mild as the West Coast variety. They were plump, slightly saline, and a delicate ivory color—

---

*By the way, it's not pronounced "CA-rol" like a flight attendant for Spirit Airlines. It's "ca-ROLE," like a sylph prancing around the Tuileries Garden.
†We spoke French, but I'll write our dialogue in English.

Goldilocks approved. In the afternoon glow, hungry and happy, we got to know each other. She was from Marseille, in the south, and lived in Paris for work. I showed her the list of places I planned to visit on my restaurant bender.

"Wow," she said. "You're going to all of these places?"

"Yeah. By the way, you're free to join me on whichever one you want to join me on."

I stayed in Paris for seven days and ate every meal with Carole. A culinary renaissance was burgeoning in the city at the time, and a new breed of restaurants and wineries was turning away from the past and stepping into an unknown future. It seemed appropriate: I was trying to do the same thing with my personal life.

We started at Le Verre Volé, the restaurant responsible for this revolution. It's known as Paris's first natural wine bar. Natural wine is both a movement and a wine. It's wine that has been messed with as little as possible. Organic, biodynamic, all the buzzwords. Some of the process is very out there. Here's a quick quiz. Which one of these practices of natural winemaking is false? (1) They plant, weed, and harvest based on patterns of the moon, (2) they fill animal horns with cow manure and bury them in the ground for six months to create a superintense fertilizer, or (3) they spray crops with nettle tea. Tricked ya! They're all true. Yup. Even the shit horn.

But the intention is noble—to make wines that are as natural as possible. I had never tried natural wine before and didn't know much about it. I love wine. A lot. But I was only used to the old-school, conventional stuff. Appropriately, my first glass was a Beaujolais. The Beaujolais region is where the natural wine movement started. In the seventies, French wines were becoming more and more mass-produced, which led, you may remember, to Beaujolais Nouveau, swill not meant for aging that came out every year, a marketing ploy to unload shitty Gamay grapes.

And because the beloved terroir of the old-school wine-growers in the region was getting worldwide recognition for such liquid garbage, they decided to band together—four main growers now known as the Gang of Four. They vowed to restore Beaujolais's status as a great wine, representing the way wines should taste—lower alcohol content, minimal intervention, letting the fruit and terroir speak for themselves. It was a long play, but fifty years later, Beaujolais is the capital of natural winemaking, and the Gamay grape, once scorned, is filling some of the most sought-after bottles on earth. They're bright, juicy, and refreshing.

Le Verre Volé, however, is way more than just a wine bar. The food was wild. Not at all what you would expect at a French restaurant. A plate of five fried sardines with a dipping sauce hit the table. It looked more appropriate to a Spanish seaside taverna than an avant-garde establishment. Crispy, fishy, a perfect mix with the yolky buttery concoction that accompanied it. Next came beef with thinly sliced sunchokes and an herb sauce. No fuss, no slick presentation, but definitely somehow French.

It was pretty magical, as was my dinner partner. Carole was a perfect culinary compatriot. Adventurous, curious, emotionally moved by food. She was as excited to go on this ride as I was.

The next night we ate at Le Chateaubriand. Our tasting menu lasted two hours. A hotshot Basque chef was cooking his take on French food. It was weird, whimsical, and the presentations were unreal. We started with little glass cups of a grapefruit-colored liquid in which a green cube bobbed like a buoy. Ceviche juice with avocado. A dazzling way to start a meal. Next came fried baby shrimp in their shells, dusted with raspberry powder. The dish was creative and bold, with the look and consistency of raspberry Cap'n Crunch. You'd pop them in whole and they'd crunch loudly, filling your mouth with flavors that would never meet in nature. Shrimpy raspberry Pop Rocks. Mind blown.

Next was a fish course: Saint-Pierre, a white fish, topped with roasted fennel and fresh cheese, doused in a dill and marjoram sauce. Sublime. Cheese and fish are not supposed to go with each other, but neither are fucking shrimp and raspberry powder. Rules are checked at the door at Chateaubriand, and merci for that.

The meat course was a roasted Iberico pork served with mixed vegetables. Iberico is rarely cooked. It's that most special of porcine ingredients that comes from special black pigs called pata negra. They roam the Spanish forests, feeding on fresh acorns. Their meat is mostly consumed cured—in my opinion, the finest example of cured pork around, better than French charcuterie, better than prosciutto di Parma. The undisputed king of cured piggy goodness.

The color of the meat is a deep burgundy, slick with a fat that is nutty and perfumed, evocative of truffles. However, when it's cooked, it is an altogether different experience. Like taking sushi-grade toro and making canned tuna out of it— sinfully perfect. Outside of barbecue, I don't really love cooked pork—too dry and bland. Not cooked Iberico. It's velvety unctuousness: tender, fatty, savory. And the simply labeled "mixed vegetables" were peas, lima beans, onions, purple carrots—whimsically cut morsels of cooked and raw vegetables, placed strategically on the plate with the deftness of a seasoned painter. You won't believe me when I tell you that all of this paled in comparison to one simple dish. A cup of broth. No garnish. No frills. Just a slate-colored cup, and a deep brown, mud-colored bouillon. It was a beef broth, but when we took a sip, before the look of bliss colored our faces, there was that split second of confusion. We both stared at each other in tension, then release. "Oh my god. What is this?"

This broth was, I assume, cooked-down bones and choice cuts of the cow with veggies and herbs. But that's the laziest way to describe it. This broth tasted of the cow's soul. It was the fullest expression of beef I had ever savored, nourishing, comforting, haunting bovine ecstasy. A cheese course deftly handed the baton from savory to sweet. And the dessert—a rhubarb cherry compote draped with a cumulonimbus marshmallow foam. We were eating, and living, in the clouds.

Carole called in sick to work, and we continued our adventure into this uncharted culinary universe. The more we stepped into this world, the closer we became. She was hilarious. Sometimes the idea of being with a foreigner is way more fun in theory than in execution. You miss a lot of connection due to the language gap and cultural blind spots. But we didn't skip a beat. She got my sarcasm; she could give it as well as take it. It felt like she was morphing from my food-and-drink partner into just my partner—after only two days!

By day four we were in a food-and-wine daze. Lunches and dinners seemed to blur together; sometimes we added extra mealtimes, like the day we stumbled into L'Avant Comptoir for linner. L'Avant Comptoir is a special little haunt that is hard to find, but once you do, you are rewarded with one of the cooler experiences in Paris. From the outside you see only a modest crêpe stand. Walk through the crêperie, enter a secret door, part a plastic curtain, and discover a crowded claustrophobic bar that is so small, apparently there's no room for menus. Hanging from the ceiling are placards with pictures of the food on offer. It's disorienting. You're packed in, staring up, choosing from the dizzying array of French-ish tapas while being energized by fun, loud music. We made our way to the bar and were greeted with boules of fresh bread and a bowling ball of bright yellow communal butter—a health violation in the best way possible.

"Deux verres de vin rouge s'il vous plaît," ordered Carole.

We got our wines, exchanged "santés" and a kiss, and embarked on our eccentric linner.

The music playing was not French but Mexican pop. The dishes were precious little parcels, mostly of offal and pig. The highlight was a chalky blood sausage wrapped in a thin layer of braised pork skin—a grown-up pig in a blanket. I remember asking the bartender, "Would you consider this food French?"

"Of course," he said, slightly offended. "It's very French. Why not?"

"No, it's delicious, it just doesn't seem traditional."

"So, you're saying French people aren't allowed to evolve?"

He made a good point. The French are originators, but why not be the innovators? Indeed, they did the same thing with art in the late nineteenth century, when Impressionism shook up

French society. Culinarily, this new generation of chefs was attempting to create a similar declaration with their dishes. Their ability to leave the past in the past was revelatory. I had a tendency of doing the opposite in my life, especially when it came to relationships.

My superhero power is that after a breakup, I spend the next year or so replaying the greatest hits in my head on a loop, leaving out all the duds, picking at the emotional scab left behind. This time was different. My wound was still fresh, but in this bewitching city I had never been to, with a woman seemingly perfect for me, surrounded by foods that offered tastes of a new imagination, I felt reborn, ready for the future. Also, I was drunk a lot of the time, so that helped too.

I asked Carole if she would ever entertain moving to the States.

"You should switch from wine to water," she said.

I was serious. I know I didn't really know her, but I couldn't imagine finding anyone better. Ever the relationship cynic, I nonetheless started wondering, "What if love actually does go like it does in the movies?"

The next night we went to Clown Bar: roasted pigeon with onion marmalade with radicchio; pithiviers, a warm pastry-enclosed terrine of duck, dates, and foie gras. I learned about her fractured relationship with her father.

The night after that was Aux Deux Amis: grilled sea snails with mayonnaise; poached white asparagus with smoked olives. I found out she's an amateur potter of extraordinary pieces.

Then Le Baratin: turbot sautéed in butter with porcini

mushrooms; braised veal tongue in vinaigrette. We laughed as I taught her that the Farsi word for her favorite drink means "royal penis."*

And finally, Septime: steamed mussels and leeks; poached egg with spelt, shallot, and hay broth. We started planning a trip together to her hometown of Marseille.

I saw us falling in love under the spell of each other and Paris's seductive dining aura.

After having gorged on the city's newest hippest food for a week, I decided I needed a break. I wanted old-school, le vieux Paris. Though smitten by the inventive meals we'd been having, now I craved something unabashedly conventional. A brasserie, belle époque, wood, red banquettes, white tablecloth with the paper cover on top, a maître d' with a snooty look, and traditional French comfort food. I needed Chez Georges.

The exterior is humble with light-colored wood, the windows covered with a simple lace curtain. The words RESTAURANT CHEZ GEORGES are hand-painted in a Toulouse-Lautrec font above the entrance. The place has been here for almost a hundred years, yet Carole had never heard of it. It was my last night in Paris, and we were going to enjoy some kitschy fun together. We walked from the quiet curb into a bustling dining room that was exactly what I wanted—a blast from the past.

Chez Georges is as old-school as it gets. There's nothing hip about it. No cool young French socialites in denim jackets and horn-rimmed glasses sipping natural wines. It's somewhat touristy, and the French people there are mostly well-dressed grandparents—at the very least dads and moms. The best way

---

*Think of that every time you drink a Kir Royale.

to date the brasserie is to know that it's one of the restaurants that made Julia Child fall in love with French cuisine when she dined on its buttery sole meunière.

A long banquette hugs the three walls, and modest square tables follow. The floors are tiny mosaics of stone that look ancient—as if they were discovered by accident when the establishment broke ground a century ago. The walls are an off-white that only age and copious amounts of nicotine can produce. The light is warm, comforting, amber, moving. High mirrors in antique wood frames arch just below the ceiling, adding to the grandeur. The maître d', a handsome older Frenchman with a full mane of gray hair, red reading glasses on a silver eyeglass chain hanging on his thick tie, told us there would be a little bit of a wait. We ordered our bottle of wine for the evening and took it outside.

We hadn't eaten much during the day in anticipation of tonight's meal, so those good grapes were hitting pretty quickly. Not only that, but we had spent the whole week drinking light, low-alcohol natural wines, and I was growing tired of twenty-year-old sommeliers in T-shirts winesplaining a movement that seemed slightly more pretentious than it was delicious.*

So we were having a high-octane Bordeaux. Outside on a chilly night we knew would be our last together, we savored every moment with the same intensity that we were savoring the syrupy gold of Château Léoville Barton. Drinking helped keep us warm. We weren't in any rush. We didn't want the night to end.

---

*Let's be honest. Outside of a handful of natural wines, most of them taste like spiked kombucha.

Eventually, the maître d' came out himself to lead us to our table, regretful about the wait. "Pas de quoi," I told him, no worries, as I lifted up our now-empty bottle of wine. "We had a friend to keep us company. And we'll take another friend, when you get a chance."

We entered arm in arm—both to be nearer to each other, and to help with balance. We were love drunk and drunk drunk.

The dining room was loud and electric. It's where older people come to let loose, which, in my opinion, is the best vibe imaginable. People ate the classics as servers dressed in black with white aprons darted around expertly tending to the house. We held hands over the table, transported to a different place and time.

With a second bottle of Bordeaux, the maître d' brought a gift from the house: "We apologize for the wait. Please have some gougères, our compliments."

The gougères were perfect little savory cream puffs oozing with cheese instead of cream. Warm pillows of melted gooey-ness that enveloped your mouth in a textural and sensual dance of dairy and yeastiness. Unfortunately, bliss was not the only thing they evoked. They were a Proustian portal back to my last relationship. Substitute these cheese balls for madeleines— gougères were Katie's favorite food.

I expected this restaurant to transport me to a different time and place, but I should have been more specific with the travel gods. My mind flew to Katie's last birthday. Before she was diagnosed with celiac disease, her favorite food had been gougères. She later lamented never being able to eat them again. On her birthday, I had woken up early, and while she slept I made a sheet pan of gougères for her from scratch. I had been working on a gluten-free recipe for a few weeks in secret and came up with the perfect blend of flours to re-create her favorite dish. I put them in a basket lined with a cloth napkin and brought them back to bed, waiting for the intoxicating smell to bring her out of her slumber. Her face was priceless—it started off captivatingly peaceful, then with a twitch of her button nose, her alluring hazel eyes opened with blissful shock as she processed her mouthwatering alarm clock.

"Wait. Are these? Gougères?"

"Yes they are."

"Gluten-free?"

"Absolutely."

We lay down in bed and popped GFGs, as she called them, and coffee, the perfect start to her birthday.

"Is everything okay?" asked Carole.

"Yeah," I said, "everything's cool. Why?"

"You seem off."

"Nope. All good."

I shielded my face with the big crystal goblet. I thought more wine could make me feel better, but everything became worse. Carole had the sole; I had the steak frites with mustard cream sauce. I couldn't tell you how it tasted because I wasn't there. I had lost my appetite—both for the food and for the fantasy. My scab-picking superpower had been released, and poor Carole had a front row seat to it.

"Dan, qu'est-ce qu'il se passe?"

"Sorry, Carole, I'm just a little sad. The gougères reminded me of something."

"Of what?"

"Nothing. How's the fish?"

"Good. What are you thinking of, Dan?" She spoke with concern.

"I'm thinking of my last relationship. I'm sorry. It's fine and it'll be over in a second."

I took another sip of wine.

"Dan, it's okay. What was your ex's name?"

"No, Carole. I don't want to ruin our last meal."

But it was too late. We skipped dessert, even though Chez Georges had the most dramatic mille-feuille on display—probably the only one I've ever seen that's actually true to the name: a thousand layers of crispy golden pastry sheets, interspersed with generous layers of cream, dense with black dots of fresh vanilla bean. Google a picture of it and you'll be as close to eating it as I was.

For the first time we left a restaurant without locking arms, unbalanced, forced to stabilize solo. As much as the city tried, with its mesmerizing cobblestone paths, streetlamps showering us with their magical glow, and intoxicating chilled scents of a Paris winter night, my mind looped through the greatest hits album of my past relationship.

Carole stopped and took my hand in hers. "I'm going to go home, okay?"

"But . . . it's my last night here."

She kissed me on the cheek, caring.

"Tu n'as toujours pas tourner la page."

You haven't yet turned the page.

She was right. One last embrace and we went our separate ways. I had gone to Paris to forget about my past, but she managed to hop a last-minute flight to meet up.

And I loved Carole. I really did. Or, fine, I loved the idea of her. And I refuse to use the word "rebound" because that cheapens the whole experience, but the truth is, I was still single a year after I met her in New York, and I never thought of visiting her. Even Carole, now a good friend, calls it a rebound. Reminiscing over Zoom recently, she summed it up nicely: "We had fun, but you were fucked up." When I agreed and jokingly offered to come back to Paris with my healed heart, she laughed. "That was the craziest week of eating and drinking in my life. Don't come back; I'm still full."

11

FEELS ON WHEELS

BACK FROM PARIS, I WAS LEFT WITH VERY LITTLE IN THE WAY OF DIS-tractions. Pain, guilt, and regret rushed to fill the void. I started to hate the person I had become and the mistakes I kept making—holding food above all else. I had acted shamefully in my past relationship and I was having a tough time facing that reality. Staying home and drinking under the guise of "I'm really getting into wine tasting" was leading me to a dark place.* I forced myself to be more social, and because my immediate friends were sick of my drama, I called Byron to see if he wanted to grab a drink.

Byron was a writer on *Kickin' It* and is partly responsible for

---

*Although I can now tell the difference between Barolo, Brunello, and Barbaresco. Also, hot tip: Tears falling into your wineglass only enhance the flavor.

giving birth to Falafel Phil. He's hilarious and positive and fun. He's also a devout Catholic. I was always fascinated by him because I know a couple of really religious people, and they're rarely the ilk I like to be around. I always feel like I have to be a more buttoned-up version of myself. Not with Byron. We have mostly a work relationship. We share scripts, exchange career advice, complain about not getting jobs, etc. We never get very personal, but I was running out of people to vent to and poor Byron was next in line.

I said I was having a hard time getting over this relationship. My coping mechanisms weren't working.

"So what have you been doing?"

"Therapy, food, wine, sex."

"And none of that's working?"

"No."

"The therapy?"

"That's working the least. I can go to a therapist for anything, and once I tell them I have a dead brother, their eyes widen, like 'Oooh, dead brother is enough sessions to build that deck I've been putting off.'"

"I mean, you know wine and sex aren't going to work, but as a married man, I'd like to hear about them in as much detail as possible, please."

"You got it."

"Okay. I know you're gonna give me shit for this, but what about giving back? Have you tried that?"

"Here we go," I said. "Gather round, ladies and gentlemen, it's time for Jesus Talk with Byron."

"Well, your people killed him so the least you could do is listen."

"Ha ha, good point."

We clinked our Scotch glasses.

"I do Meals on Wheels every Saturday morning. I've been doing it for thirteen years. It's nothing religious. It'll be good for your soul. We drive around L.A. and give meals to people who need it, via our wheels. At the very least it's a good hang, and the characters are priceless."

"I don't know, it's not really my thing."

"Look, your thing has been going all over eating and fucking your face off to feel better, and it hasn't worked. Maybe you need to bring meals to others rather than seeking them yourself."

"Oh, you're so fucking poetic."

"I'll see you Saturday. I can't wait to hear all about your dead brother."

"Ha. What time?"

"Nine A.M."

"No way, dude, I'm gonna be hungover as shit. Can't they wait until the afternoon?"

"It's for people who have no way of getting out of the house to get food."

"Okay, so they literally can't go anywhere. Let's roll up at three. Intermittent fasting can be good for them."

"Just don't drink one fucking Friday of your life, degenerate."

Hungover at nine the next Saturday morning, but filled with newfound knowledge of Austrian Rieslings, I drove to a soup kitchen in a gritty part of L.A. The parking lot held these endearing Meals on Wheels vans—a cross between a mail truck and an ice cream truck, with angel wings on the back.

Byron met me in the parking lot wearing a green Meals on Wheels shirt.

"Well, well, well, look who's going to do good for a change."

"Fuck you. I just want one of those shirts so I can wear it out and people think I'm a good person."

"Unfortunately, you get one."

"For real?"

"Yeah, come in, you have to do some paperwork too." Then he handed me a hairnet and booties. "Put these on. We go through the kitchen to get to the office."

The industrial kitchen had cauldrons aplenty, a lot of stainless steel, large red tiles—it was very reminiscent of a high school cafeteria. Everything was overly sanitary like you would imagine a kitchen full of oversight to be. Enormous chunks of meat machine-wrapped in plastic, the ventilator roaring like a jet engine. The "chef de cuisine" if you will, a stocky man in his forties, seemed way too young to be walking with a cane, but there he was, limping from stockpot to stockpot, steaming up his wire-framed glasses as he checked in on his concoctions.

"What up, Reggie!"

"Byron, what's going on?"

"This is my good friend Dan."

"How are you, Dan the man?"

"Great, Reggie. What's on the menu?"

"Pork with green beans and mashed potatoes."

"What about for the Jews?"

"We don't feed the Jews," said Byron.

I loved this place.

I met the nun in charge, an older Black woman named Sister Daphne. She was sitting at her desk in her office, struggle-typing, squinting her eyes behind bifocals. Also, nuns have offices.

"Sister Daphne, this is my good friend Dan."

She rose to greet us with a sweet smile. The kind you can't help but mirror.

"Well, hello, Dan. Welcome."

"Hello, Sister. I believe you may be the first sister I've ever met."

"You've never met a Black woman before?"

A nun with a sense of humor!

We filled out my paperwork and she handed me my T-shirt.

"You're doing God's work, Dan. Thank you so much for being here."

The way she said it gave me goosebumps, so I made a joke, which is what I do when I feel uncomfortable.

"I don't know about that, I'm just trying to get some free food."

Sister Daphne suddenly got dead serious.

"No you are not," she said, hitting every syllable. Then she smiled again. "Have a blessed day, you two."

She sat back in her chair as Byron and I exited her office.

"That was intense," I said.

"She's like that. She has a great sense of humor, but hates the self-deprecating stuff."

"Cool, so my whole vibe."

"Basically."

We made it back to the van and started to pack the backseat with huge coolers filled with packaged meals. I got into the passenger side seat and Byron handed me a clipboard.

"Before we do anything, we need temperatures of the hot

food to make sure it's safe from bacteria," he said. "I'll do this, and you just mark the meals with a checkmark once I tell you."

"Got it."

"Start handing me trays."

I reached back and opened a cooler. I pulled out the first shrink-wrapped tray from the stack and handed it to Byron. Each tray was split in little sections. Byron pierced the plastic with the thermometer and inserted it into the gelatinous blob of pork, waiting for the temperature numbers to finally stop their steady climb.

"One hundred sixty-five for Mr. Martinez."

I checked the box next to Mr. Martinez.

"Got it."

This went on until all fifteen names were completed.

By now, the van smelled porcine—a foul odor, like how your kitchen would smell if you left pork sitting on the counter overnight. I rushed to open my window as we started on our way.

The first stop was Mr. Martinez. "Ready for your first client?"

Staring at the four-unit building that was built during the Vietnam War and had aged about as gracefully as that conflict has, I replied, "Absolutely not."

"Great." Then reading from the clipboard: "No restrictions. So just grab a regular tray, one milk, and one juice."

I grabbed Mr. Martinez's meal and was ready to head out when Byron stopped me.

"Just so you know, he's a hoarder, so it's going to take a while for him to come to the door, but he'll be there. Oh, also he has a glass eye."

"Really?"

"Yeah. I felt like you should know so that you don't act surprised when you see it."

"Good looking out.* So I just hand it to him?"

"For him, yes. For others, they want you to bring it inside and set it on a specific table or something."

"Got it."

"One more thing. Keep in mind that for many of them, this is the only time of the week they're having any human interaction, and that's sometimes as important as the food."

"Okay. Glass eye, just hand it to him, be cordial. Anything else?"

"You're good, homie."

I opened the van door and set out into the great unknown. It felt surreal, like I was trespassing. I was, first off, in a neighborhood I would never otherwise encounter, and now I was maneuvering the labyrinth of a rundown building I would never otherwise visit, looking for unit 2A.

The shades were completely drawn, and I could hear the TV muffled in the background. I rang the bell and waited, as I was told. About three minutes later, not exaggerating, Mr. Martinez finally opened the door of the six-hundred-square-foot one-bedroom.

I didn't even notice the imposing man at the door because the sheer volume of matter piled up in his apartment overwhelmed me. It was like he was living in an overfilled storage facility for every flea market that ever existed. Towers of junk

---

*To my credit, I did *not* say "no pun intended."

reached to the ceiling, leaving a labyrinth just big enough for one person to squeeze through.

"Hello, young man!" he said, in a heavy Mexican accent, bringing my eyes back to him. He did indeed have a glass eye. However, what Byron had failed to mention was that the glass eye was a different color from his real eye! Not completely different, like those dogs, just a different shade of brown, which seemed even more strange.

"Mr. Martinez, here's your pork."

"Ahh. Puerca. Thank you."

"You got it." I tried to use the TV sounds to extend the conversation a little.

"So what are you watching?"

"Television. Okay, thank you, thank you."

And he closed the door on me.

"Cool, cool, cool."

I got back into the van.

"Congrats, brother! First one. How did it go?"

"It was good. He was nice. Kind of weird. Also, you should've told me one of his eyes was a different shade of the same color."

"I gotta leave some surprises for you."

"His eyes looked like one of those paint sample cards for brown."

"Ha! That's messed up."

By now you're probably thinking Byron is, like, saintly. He does charity, he brings his friends in on the act, he's charming and fun, so let me burst that bubble—he has awful road rage. We're in this charity mobile and he's cutting people off, he's giving the finger to people who cut us off, he's yelling and honking at people who don't proceed immediately when the light turns green. "Go, fucker!" He's making illegal U-turns, blowing through stop signs and questionable yellow/red lights, to which he responds, "There's no way a cop is going to give a ticket to the fucking Meals on Wheels van."* This detail isn't super pertinent to the chapter, but I'm tired of having myself look bad and everyone else look good, so this is purely to bring him down a notch so you see my virtue by comparison.

We pulled up to another tired apartment building.

"You're gonna love this one. Marnie Koeppel. She's a woman in her eighties, lives alone, and she always answers the door wearing a robe that's open, and she's naked."

"Shut the fuck up."

"I swear."

"I don't believe you."

Byron consulted the clipboard. "She's low sodium."

I stared at him a beat, and he gave me a "you'll see" look. I fished out a tray from the low-sodium bin.

Each meal is organized by dietary restriction. There's low sodium, low sugar, no sodium, no sugar, no pork, no beef, no pork or beef, vegetarian, no dairy. The actual contents of the tray didn't seem to matter nearly as much as what was omitted.

I called on the intercom, and a frail old lady, after a throat clearing, answered.

"Yes, hello?"

"Hi, Meals on Wheels."

---

*And he's right! We got pulled over once for an illegal U-turn and he told the cop he had a new client on the list and that he wasn't familiar with the address. The cop let us go. So now he's a road rager *and* a liar.

Bzzzzzzzzz.

I walked down the hall, nervous with excitement. I knocked on her door and heard footsteps coming toward me.

After unlocking twelve dead bolts, Marnie opened the door.

Marnie had short, well-coiffed gray hair. She wore wire-framed glasses over her glittery sunken eyes, which were exactly level with mine. Her librarian's face was chock-full of wrinkles, and she smiled wide with excitement.

"Well, hello, dear."

Also, she was naked. Fully fucking naked. Save for a ratty crêpe robe that was hanging on the far outskirts of her shoulders, everything was on view.

I beamed. "Well, hello to you!"

"It looks chilly outside."

"Yeah, it's a little chilly."

"They say on the news it's going to last a few more days, and then we should be back in the seventies."

I couldn't stop smiling. "Isn't that great."

I had never seen a naked eighty-year-old woman before, let alone one just nonchalantly nude while talking to me. I was fascinated. She was neither coquettish nor self-conscious. It was somehow the most civilized inappropriate scene I had ever been a part of.

"Would you like to take the food, or should I drop it off somewhere?"

"Oh, I'll take it."

Arms outstretched, she grabbed the tray, her breasts . . . doing what they did.

"Thank you, dear, do you mind getting the door?"

"Not at all. You enjoy, Mrs. Koeppel."

"Oh, please," she said, her covered back to me. "Call me Marnie."

"Keep it casual, sure. Take care, Marnie."

I closed the door and stood mouth agape. In the van, Byron nodded his head with a devilish grin.

"I told you."

"I mean, I don't know what to say. That was one of the craziest things that's ever happened to me."

"She's a sweetheart, though, right?"

"The sweetest! That's what made it so weird."

"These people are all like family to me. I'm glad you get to meet them."

What a good guy Byron is, I thought. Then he honked at a woman with a stroller not crossing the road fast enough. We got on the freeway, and a few miles later he exited on Sunset Boulevard.

"West Hollywood?"

"Yeah, the next guy, Angel, lives on Curson and Sunset."

"What? That's a block away from me."

"It's not just poor people who get Meals on Wheels; it's for people who just can't take care of themselves and have no family or help. Sad, lonely people who are stuck. You'd be an ideal recipient, actually."

We pulled up to Angel's place. It was a nice charming little bungalow.

"You're gonna love this guy; he curses a lot, but in a weird way. Like, the curse words are out of place. You'll see. He's low sodium."

I grabbed a low-sodium pork, juice, and milk, and walked up to the bungalow. Angel is ninety-one years old, a five-foot-tall portly Cuban, confidently sporting funky thick-frame glasses, a short-sleeved button-down shirt, and linen pants. He looked cool. He greeted me at the door.

"Hello, my friend."

"Hi, Angel."

"Where's Mr. Byron?"

"He's in the van."

He looked over and waved.

"Hey, Byron!"

"What up, Angel?"

"I'm good. Just fucking watching the fucking football game later." Definitely one "fuck" too many. What made the comment especially weird is that he delivered his profanity with a huge nonchalant grin on his face.

"What's your name, my friend?"

"I'm Dan."

"Nice to fucking meet you, Dan."

"Yeah, nice to fucking meet you too, Angel."

I handed him his tray, and he took a deep inhale.

"This shit smells delicious," he said.

"Indeed, it does," I said as he slunk into his home and softly closed the door.

Back in the van, Byron was marking the clipboard, figuring out our remaining route.

"The best, right?"

"What a character. These guys are all something."

"They're great. Next up is Mrs. Winchell and her son, Carl."

We drove a few blocks down to an Eastern Bloc–looking complex that housed a low-income community of predominantly elderly Russian tenants. I grabbed two low-sodium/

low-sugar trays and made my way into the courtyard. Suspicious Soviet octogenarians eyed me from behind windows as I made my way to Mrs. Winchell. I waved hello to a grizzled old man on a walker and got back an angry grunt as he lurched toward me, his walker thudding as loudly as the tennis balls on the legs allowed.

With an enormous "Hello, handsome," Mrs. Winchell, a sunbeam of a large Black woman, opened the door. She smiled so wide, her cheeks seemed permanently etched in a grin. "Come inside, come inside," she said, waving, and I followed her and her bright pink furry slippers. How she came to penetrate this iron curtain of an old folks home, I have no idea.

The apartment was small and cluttered, poorly lit. The smell of bacon was dense and only getting more overwhelming as we walked through a dark hallway to the dingy rundown kitchen. This was the hub of the home. A tiny TV was blaring *The Price Is Right,* and a heavyset man in his thirties was sitting at the small kitchen table on a folding chair, bent over an open Bible, scanning intensely, his tongue protruding with the effort. Next to the prominent Bible was a stack of index cards for note-taking.

"Put them right over there, handsome," said Mrs. Winchell.

I set the trays on the counter and couldn't help but notice the enormous cast-iron skillet so full of bacon it was draping over the sides, like it was going to be the crust for a pie. There was an open bag of Cheetos and unopened two-liter bottles of Shasta stacked on the top of the cabinets, the sink stuffed to capacity.

"Here you go, Mrs. Winchell," I said, eyeing the shrine of

sizzling bacon. "No salt, no sugar," I said just sarcastically enough to go over her head.

"Thank you, handsome. Say hello, Carl."

Carl snapped out of his biblical hypnosis and stood up.

He stuttered, "Hello."

"Hi, Carl. Nice to meet you."

"Nice to meet you too," he replied, and reached for the closest index card. "Here you go. Have a blessed day," he said laboriously as he handed me a quote from the Bible.

"Thanks, Carl. You have a blessed day too."

I walked back to Byron, brandishing my index card.

"You got a quote!" he said. "What did you get?"

"'He who killeth the Jew shall inherit the earth.'"

"That's why they call it the Good Book."

"'Be kind and compassionate to one another, forgiving each other, just as in Christ God forgave you. Ephesians 4:32.'"

"He walks around the neighborhood and hands people Bible quotes."

"That's kind of adorable."

"Also, don't feel special that Mrs. Winchell called you handsome. She calls everyone handsome."

"Wow, what a dick. You couldn't just let me have that?"

"Okay, last stop is Darren Siegel."

Byron pulled an illegal U-turn, and we headed up into the hills. We were in one of the fanciest neighborhoods in Los Angeles—just behind the famed Chateau Marmont Hotel.

"Who the hell is Darren Siegel?" I asked, as we passed mansion after mansion.

"Ninety-six-year-old gay dude. Used to be one of the biggest dance choreographers in Hollywood. He has the craziest stories about how he used to play golf with Sinatra and party with that crew. Apparently, there's a street named after the guy; he's a trip."

And yet, he was having a supplemented lunch of bland pork, low on the sodium.

I walked up to the home, which was large without being ostentatious, classic midcentury modern. The house was great, but the view was like nothing I had ever seen. The home perched on a cliff overlooking a full panoramic shot of Los Angeles from the ocean to the skyscrapers. The type of view that screams "I run this fucking town!" This was easily a seven-million-dollar home.*

I rang the doorbell, hypnotized.

"Meals on Wheels!"

I heard a deep, regal voice say, "Right away." Not what I'd expect from someone his age.

And entering stage right was a lithe, tall, handsome man who, though lacking synovial fluid in his joints, had the same swagger and grace dancers have no matter their age. He opened the screen.

He stared at me through amber-coated glasses under a faded navy-blue bucket hat.

"Well, you're not Byron." He had one of those old-timey radio voices.

"He's in the van. I'm Dan."

He tipped his hat. "Darren. A pleasure."

"The . . . pleasure is all mine. Your view is stunning."

---

*Probably nine mil by the time this book is out.

"I've lived here for longer than I can remember, and it still doesn't get old. I'm a lucky man."

"Right," I thought, as I glanced at the anemic food warming my hands.

"Well, here's your lunch." I handed him the tray.

"What are we having today?"

"Pork with some green beans and mashed potatoes."

"Ah. Lovely," he said, gracefully dipping his nose for a whiff.

I tried my best to take an inventory of the home while the door was open. It looked like an *Architectural Digest* spread from the sixties frozen in time. Green shag carpeting, Eames chairs, *Jetsons*-looking chandelier. The vestiges of a gloried past.

"Thank you, Dan. You have a nice day."

He walked his lunch to a table by the window to eat bland volunteer food in front of a million-dollar view.

When we had dropped off all the food, I was left with so much to digest. My mind was flooded with new characters who seemed a world away in circumstance, yet some literally lived on my block. Some encounters were heartbreaking, some uplifting, and some baffling. A heavy day. At the very least, though, it distracted me from obsessing over my last relationship. I went an entire morning without thinking about Katie and my failings for the first time since the breakup, which seemed like a win.

I went back every week and got closer and closer with the people on our route. They started to know me by name; I felt more comfortable and would crack jokes as I dropped off chicken Kiev, enchiladas, low-sodium beef. I'd ask how the food was the week prior and would bask in their Yelp reviews. "Oh, the enchiladas were fine, Dan." Seems like a mundane review until you hear it delivered by a naked eighty-year-old woman.

I also became more at ease in their spaces. I no longer thought of their homes as tired or grim, like I did at first. The trips became less heavy. I stopped trying to extract some higher meaning from the situation and just started to enjoy the ride. My clients became less like cartoon characters and more like kooky buddies that I'd drop in on for a quick hang. I started to feel their presence on days I didn't work. They were all over the city, so almost anywhere I drove, I passed a client or two, a brief flash inspiring a smile or a chuckle.

Then I could bask in their small victories. Mr. Martinez watched *Judge Judy* all day, and he would try to guess who would win and lose before each case. "Dan, today I guessed five of five right," he said, jubilant. "Well done, señor." "I can tell just by looking at them. For ejemplo, when the Black guys they are on, I know—" "Okay, Mr. Martinez, I have to go."

Marnie showed up in a brand-new robe one Saturday, and she was beaming. "New robe!" I said. "Yes, my daughter in Maine bought it for me," she said, as she moved her shoulders back and forth, modeling it. "Well, you looked wonderful in the last one, and even more wonderful in this one," I said, as I handed her the tray of chicken cordon bleu. Yup. Still very naked, but now that I knew her, I saw the robe less as a goofy accoutrement and more as the talisman that turned her into Super Marnie.

Angel met a woman at his salsa night who was "very fucking sweet."

Mrs. Winchell's son, Carl, stuttered less with me every week. He even tried to make me his missionary, giving me a small stack of Bible quotes to hand out to the other people on our route. Carl, if you're reading this, I never gave them to anyone. I didn't think it would be professional. Please forgive me. In fact, look to Ephesians 4:32 for guidance.

Riding with Byron was cleansing. He turned our Meals on Wheels van into a mobile confessional booth where I could unload all of my guilt and shame to him. I offered up the nastiest things I could think about myself, and Byron would temper my harshness in a judgment-free, albeit road-rage-filled, zone.

Once when I was lamenting about the way I had treated Katie, he gave me some advice that I'll never forget.

"You know how everyone gives Christians shit for this concept of original sin? Like, why should you make a kid feel guilty even though he didn't really do anything? I think there's a better interpretation. It's more about normalizing sin. It's a way of saying, as a human you're going to make mistakes. There's no way around it. Rather than beating yourself up, just know that what you did was part of the human condition. So be nicer to yourself. You're human," he said, as he made an illegal right turn on red. "See?" he said with a smile. "It's all good. I'm human."

I was so used to religion's strictness, wielded like a hammer. But Byron's brand of religiosity, an innate compassion and an attempt to understand other people,* felt great at a time when I was losing faith in myself and in my other religion—food. The whole experience was rocking my definition of what food

---

*So long as they're not driving a car.

meant. I'd been so busy seeking the greatest meals to make me feel better, and here were people eating food that was pure sustenance, and they were filled with gratitude for simple blessings that didn't require a reservation three months in advance. A new robe, a hot meal, a warm interaction with a stranger on the porch—these were their treasures. If only I could look at life with the same perspective they had. If only I could focus less on the undercooked risotto of the tasting menu, and more on the eleven splendid dishes that surrounded it.

One day we were doing our route, ending with Darren. By this time we were friendly. He knew I was a comedian, and would tell me stories of Old Hollywood roasts he had attended at the Friars Club, and how he had partied with Don Rickles and the Rat Pack, as I handed him low-sodium tuna fish salad. This time he took his tray and said, "Merci." I responded, "De rien." "Tu parles français?" he said. "Bien sûr," I said.

I told him that a few months back I had taken a food tour of Paris. Hang on, he said, and hurried off to a recess of the home. A few minutes later he came back with a yellowed signed framed menu from Paul Bocuse's groundbreaking restaurant in Lyon.

"I was working in Paris when Bocuse received three Michelin stars and was on a train to Lyon the next day."

"Are you kidding me? You went to Bocuse in 1965?!"

"I sure did. It was glorious."

I was shocked. Going to Paul Bocuse in 1965 is like seeing Babe Ruth at . . . some really important game he played—I'm not a sports guy. Regardless, it is the holy grail of restaurant eating, and Darren, a Meals on Wheels client, had been there.

As Darren took his tray and walked to his spot, I couldn't

help seeing my Ghost of Foodie Future. Here was a man who had eaten at the best restaurants in the world and now was alone and happy to fill the last remaining years of his belly with tasteless tuna. This man was savvy about cuisine. Why didn't he move mountains to get better food? How could he be happy eating this grub, knowing what else was out there, and knowing he had the means to somehow procure it? Sell your house! Downsize and hire a chef to cook the best low-sodium meals for you every single day!

I know. That's a lot to ask of a ninety-six-year-old. But still . . . Darren didn't tie happiness to food, which made zero sense to me. Did he have some great epiphany one day that set him straight? Was it age and/or gratitude for making it another day? Or maybe for Darren, food and happiness were never linked as fiercely as they were for me. He was the normal one. Why was I so fucked up?

As a child, I played a food game—discerning the flavors, discovering the best—with my dad, which he then abandoned. But the game was the only thing that ever brought me attention, so I got really good at it. So much so that anyone who couldn't play by my rules or didn't value the exploration seemed to be rejecting me like my dad did. When he started to pray three times a day, so did I. My religion, though, was breakfast, lunch, and dinner, three daily chances to affirm my worth through appreciation and understanding of food.

I thought my judgment would help me find love instead of fending it off. If I applied that harsh judgment to myself, good fortune would recognize my worth. Instead, I kept climbing a food ladder, head focused on the summit, allowing partners to join me only if they could help me climb higher, and ruthlessly rejecting anyone who couldn't keep up, no matter how perfect they were.

Well, now I was at the top of the ladder and awaiting me was a medal podium surrounded by empty bleachers. I saw the cruelty of this game, that it was fixed from the beginning. The only worthy partner had retired from the field, and nobody else could ever match up. I saw at last that it was time for me to stop playing. My dad had a new game he had to play to survive the loss of his son. I needed to respect that rather than throw hedonic tantrums in protest.

By stepping off the podium and taking my seat in the bleachers, I could appreciate the game without the harsh intensity of being a participant. And I could enjoy having people sit with me comfortably. I still love food, but it no longer needs to define me or the people around me. Instead, I'm trying to play the game of my Meals on Wheels clients, taking pleasure in simple blessings. That's it. Sounds easy, but it's a much more difficult game to play. But if you get good at it, there's no Michelin-starred meal that can match up.

I haven't turned into a monk, but my food snobbery is not as intense. It's mellowed out, buffed down. It's no longer my mission to make every meal an adventure, nor do I go into a downward spiral when I eat something subpar. I used to be militant about trying a new place every night, but now I have two regular joints that I rarely stray from—Marvin and Nanbankan. I go less for the food (although it's great) and more for the place. Good restaurants aren't the ones winning all the awards; they're the ones creating a nourishing community through food where anyone can play. The warm hug on the way in, spirited conversations with regulars and staff, the complimentary digestif after I've paid my bill. These culinary creature comforts matter so much more than the food. In that way, I've become less a patron and more like one of the clients on my route.

Also, it's not like all of the adventure has been taken out of my eating. In fact, I'm writing this last chapter in Mexico City, where I've been eating some of the best food I've ever had in my life.* But I've had some duds too, and it no longer leaves me indignant about a meal opportunity lost. Don't get me wrong—it bugs me, but I'm on the steady path to giving as few fucks as Marnie in her robe.

I've lived most of my life judging people by their relationship to food. Whether friends, family, or lovers,† they needed to pass a rigorous culinary obstacle course to be worthy. Meals on Wheels helped me learn how silly a yardstick that is. It's like judging someone by how many sweaters they own. I've lightened the load I place on food. It's no longer an overworked sherpa tasked with guiding me through life. It's the goofy guy on the sidelines I high-five once in a while for some extra juice. All right. Well, I can go on and on about how my attitude toward food is now in a good place, but I have a reservation at Quintonil tonight that I made three months ago and I'm not going to be late.‡

---

*I'm not posting about it on Instagram because I'm a little behind on my deadline and didn't want my editor to know that I left town on a food adventure when I should be at home focused on writing about them. Sorry, Madhulika! I'll have a mezcal in your honor tonight.
†*God,* I hate this word but, damn it, it works well in the sentence.
‡The End.

EPILOGUE

IN LATE 2019, I WAS ACTING ON A NETFLIX SERIES CALLED *THE CREW*. IT was shooting on Long Island, only miles away from where I grew up. I started to read obsessively about Covid-19 and how it was making its way from China through Europe. Eventually, it came to New York. It was super scary, and everyone in my circle was freaking out—everyone except for my parents. "Guys, do *not* go to supermarkets. I will order things for you." "Don't be such a voos," my mom would say. "Mom, promise me." "Yeah, okay, I promise," she'd say with a dismissive smile I could sense through the phone.

We shut down production, and since most of the cast lived in Los Angeles, we started to plan our return. I packed all my stuff in an Uber and headed to the airport. I called my mom on the way, and a few seconds into the conversation I heard a beep in the background that sounded like a cash register.

"Mom, where are you?"

"Nowhere, don't worry."

"Paper or plastic, ma'am?" said a voice in the background.

"Plastic," my mom whispered. "Okay, Dan joon, have a safe flight."

"Mom, where the hell are you?"

"At the supermarket."

"What are you doing at the supermarket?"

"I needed dill! Leave me alone."

She went to the supermarket . . . for dill . . . and only dill!

I was beside myself. I rerouted my Uber to my parents' house. If I took off, I felt, they were going to get Covid and die. So rather than return to L.A., I spent the first three months of the pandemic living at home, as a forty-year-old man, with my parents.

Up until this point, my food relationship with my parents had pretty much devolved to novelty. I would come back to New York once in a while, eat a meal or two at home, then go to Manhattan with friends to try the fun new places all the other nights.

I went from having no food relationship with my parents to having every single meal with them. My mom and I would start every morning recipe planning for the day. My dad would give us his order, then we'd usually roll our eyes and make whatever we wanted. It started out slightly charged. I would say things like "Mom, maybe let's try to make the roast chicken with za'atar instead of cumin." And in her charming accent she'd say something supportive like "You are really stupid, you know that?" But after establishing who the alpha was (her), we got into a groove. We were trying out new recipes: I would teach her a couple of moves, she would teach me some, then we'd sit at the table with my dad and eat. Three meals a day, for three months. And you know what? We had a blast. We usually had a Persian frittata, called "kuku," at the ready. It was made with whatever vegetables and herbs we could get our hands on, onions, garlic, and a dash of turmeric. We made weird Persian dishes that neither of us had ever made before, like sarsheer, a Middle Eastern clotted cream, and nan-e nokhodchi, tiny chickpea flour cookies that are shaped like clovers. We made bread (I know, basic); we infused grappa with rosemary; we started "happy hour" as soon as the sun came down; we had wonderful dinners, then played cards until bedtime. We made up for lost time. All the meals I skipped out on because of my hang-ups were suddenly being eaten. All the laughs we missed out on were laughed. All the conversations about the past were finally filled in over a fragrant home-cooked meal.

Those few months gave us a lot of fun memories. We actually created what became one of the most viral videos of the early pandemic—me awkwardly watching a graphic sex scene from the show *Homeland* sitting next to my parents with the caption "Take me now, COVID." So far it has eight million views. It's my pinned tweet. Check it out @standupdan.

But my most cherished memory is of April 20, when my dad turned eighty. He is extremely social, and spending this milestone at home was hard for him. Most years he celebrated his birthday at his favorite restaurant in Manhattan, a kosher bistro called Le Marais.* The steak frites was his favorite dish, and a few days before his birthday he said in passing, "I guess I'll have to wait until my eighty-first for my steak." The hell he did.

I found one kosher butcher on Long Island that sold hanger steak, the proper cut for an authentic steak frites. I snuck away decked out in PPE to pick it up. On the night of his birthday, I asked him and my mom to go out for a walk for a half hour. I seared steaks, double-fried the fries, whipped up a chimichurri, and when they returned, on the table was a bottle of wine and three steaming sliced steak frites. Shocked, my dad gave me a strong hug, and we rejoiced, bringing Le Marais to us. He finished his last bite, shook his head, and said, "This is the best birthday dinner I've ever had." Mine was the duck confit he gave me three decades prior. I guess now we're even.

I know it wasn't the best steak frites he'd ever had, but I tried giving him the essence of a dish he thought was impossible under the circumstances. In my family, that's the highest form of love. And nothing tastes better than love.†

Finally, I kind of hate when food memoirs end chapters with recipes, but my mom risked her life for this dill rice, so it's the least I can do. I mean, I don't know that I'd say it's to *actually* die for, but it's to die for.

In fact, here is the actual transcript of the phone call I had

---

*The quality of Kosher restaurants in NY has changed dramatically since I was a kid, and Le Marais is fantastic.
†If you see me in public, please slap me for writing that sentence, even though it's true. Thank you.

with my mother, so you can see exactly what I go through whenever I need a recipe. Enjoy!

Me: Hey, Mom.

Mom: Hi, gol [flower], how are you?

Me: Great. Mom, can you help me with a recipe?

Mom: Okay—you didn't send me the link for the house you saw yesterday.

Me: I don't think I'm going to put an offer on it.

Mom: But you didn't send me the link. You said you would send me the link.

Me: Yeah, but I'm not putting an offer on it.

Mom: But send it to me. You said you would send it to me.

Me: Mom, what's the point?

Mom: I just want to see the house.

Me: I'm not even going to put an offer on it!

Mom: Relax.

Me: [deep breath] I'm relaxed. Mom. Can you help me with a recipe?

Mom: I'm at Northport [the antiques center where she has a booth]. Working.

Me: Oh, you're in Northport working. Okay.

Mom: Yeah. Yeah, I'm a working girl.

Me: You're a working girl. So . . . do you have time to give me a recipe or no?

Mom: For what?

Me: For the . . . the rice with the dill.

Mom: Oh, rice with the dill. Yes, I can give it to you.

Me: Okay. Let's go.

Mom: You don't have that ... that book? [She's referring to Najmieh Batmanglij's book *Food of Life,* which is the authority on Persian cooking.]

Me: Yes, but I want yours. I want your specific one.

Mom: Oh, you want mine. Okay. Um. You know to make any polo [rice]? Or this is your first one?

Me: I mean, I kind of know.

Mom: Okay. According to how much rice you use, you have to buy dill. You use fresh dill or dry dill?

Me: You tell me.

Mom: They both go. I like fresh dill, but they both can be used.

Me: Remember in the height of the pandemic, when you went to go get dill for your rice?

Mom: Yes. [laughs]

Me: Yeah, really funny.

Mom: Zan Dai Joon [her aunt] uses three bunches of dill for one cup of rice.

Me: Okay.

Mom: I don't do that. [laughs] That's too much dill.

[pause]

Me: Um, okay. But how much should I use?

Mom: You can use ... you know at the supermarket, the bunches are usually different amounts. There are smaller bunches, and bigger bunches, but like, a regular bunch.

Me: A regular bunch.

Mom: You can get two bunches, for two cups.

Me: Okay, got it.

Mom: And then you can use ... of course, the ideal is to have fayva beans.

Me: Fava beans.

Mom: What?

Me: Fava beans. Not fayva beans.

Mom: But if you can get that, there's—

Me: What's a fayva bean?

Mom: What?

Me: I only know fava beans.

Mom: [laughs] They are from the same family, khar [donkey].

Me: [laughing] Okay.

Mom: You can use lima beans, you can use, how do you say? Fava beans?

Me: Yep.

Mom: Or even green beans, you know, that's nice too.

Me: Okay.

Mom: And even . . . what do you call the long ones?

Me: String beans?

Mom: Yes, string beans. Cut . . . cut string beans.

Me: Okay. Let's go, let's go, back on track, Mom. I have a meeting soon.

[patron walks in]

Mom: [to patron] Hello, how are you?

Patron: [muffled]

Mom: [to patron] It's actually an Art Deco piece. Beautiful. Eighteen-karat gold. This brooch is part of a set with . . .

[three minutes later]

Mom: [to patron] Take care. [to me] Okay, so, okay. That's how you make the rice.

[pause]

Me: [frustrated] Mom, what do you mean? You just told me two cups of rice and two bunches of dill and then named five beans!

Mom: Right. Those are the ingredients. And if you keep sounding angry, I hang up on you.

Me: [deep breath]

Mom: Okay. And then, you, um, I have to tell you about how to make the rice, or you know already?

Me: I mean, you can help me a little bit.

Mom: How many times have I taught you?

Me: A lot.

Mom: And you still don't remember?

Me: I'm stupid, Mom.

Mom: John Hopkin, my foot.

Me: Johns Hopkins.

Mom: John Hopkins.

Me: Johns, not John—okay, Mom. Rice.

Mom: Okay, you . . . you put the rice, two cups of rice, wash them. And then, on top of it, add water, and add salt, and leave it for at least one, two hours. Okay?

Me: Okay.

Mom: You can do that overnight also. And then you cut . . . you wash the dill, and dry them, and cut them very, very tiny.

Me: Okay.

Mom: Okay, and if you use fava beans, it has two skins.

Me: Fayva.

Mom: Fayva, you said fava. I said fayva and you said no.

Me: No, I'm joking, it's fava bean.

Mom: [laughing] Khar [donkey]. I usually don't take the second skin off, but you can do it if you want.

Me: Okay.

Mom: And if they are big you can cut them in half. Okay?

Me: Okay.

Mom: Then you boil a lot of water. [to a colleague] I need that for Connie. Thank you. [to me] Yes, and then you boil the water, and then drain the rice that has salt on it, and put the rice in the boiling water, and you have to add a little bit salt to the water also.

Me: Okay, got it.

Mom: And then, when it starts boiling, you have to taste one or two rices, and see if it's al dente. Not very soft, and not very hard. Al dente—

Me: I know what al dente is, baby.

Mom: What?

Me: I know what al dente is, baby.

Mom: Yeah. Al dente. Then you put it in the calendar [not colander], the rice, then you put a little bit of water, a little bit of oil at the bottom of the deeg [pot]. You can add a little zarchubeh.

Me: Zarchubeh is turmeric.

Mom: Yes, yes. And then put, eh, potatoes. You want to put potatoes for tahdeeg?

Me: Of course.

Mom: Okay. Then you wash the potatoes, skin them, and cut them in round things—

Me: So I have to wash the potatoes, I can't put a dirty potato in.

Mom: No, NO dirty potatoes. [laughter] And if you do, your dad shouldn't know. Oh, by the way, he's becoming crazy with his cleaning stuff. It kills you. Kills you.

Me: [laughing] What did he do?

Mom: He just . . . I can't get into it. So . . . then you put the potatoes on the water and the oil, and put some rice over it, and make it tight.

Me: Make it tight?

Mom: Push it down. Put the rice down onto the potatoes. And then add a little dill, a little bean, then again, a little rice, a little dill, a little bean, then again, a little rice, a little—

Me: I get it, Mom.

Mom: —until you put all the rice and the dill and the things in it.

Me: Okay.

Mom: And then you cover it. Put on a . . . not very high thing. A little less than medium heat.

Me: Okay.

Mom: And after a little while, take the top off, and if it's steaming, add a little oil on top of the rice. And then close it, and put the heat less.

Me: Okay.

Mom: And it will be ready after half an hour, forty minutes.

Me: Okay. Got it.

Mom: And if you smell something burning, run.

Me: [laughing] Okay, don't turn it off, just run.

Mom: [laughing] Yes. That's it. It's not difficult.

Me: Okay, that's not difficult at all, ha ha. Thank you, Mom. I love you.

Mom: I love you too, gol. Send me the link for the house.

Me: You got it.

You know what? Just google Najmieh Batmanglij's recipe for Persian Rice with Fava Beans and Dill.

ACKNOWLEDGMENTS

WRITING A BOOK WAS THE HARDEST THING I'VE EVER DONE, AND NEVER something I envisioned doing. If not for my immensely smart rock star of a manager, Eryn Brown at Entertainment 360, this book would not have happened. She heard me on Steve Rinella's podcast and urged me to turn my stories into chapters. Thanks for believing in the unbelievable. Wine soon, please.

Liz Parker, my agent at Verve, took those chapters and ran with them. Liz, you are a force. Thanks for taking a chance on a first-time writer and championing this project. Serious publishers read my chapters, and I know it's just because they came from you. Negronis soon, please. (I'm realizing I drink a lot with my reps.)

Madhulika Sikka, my editor at Crown Publishing, decided to hitch her wagon to mine and go on this adventure together.

You were new to the company and took me on as one of your first authors. Your guidance helped give an arc to a bunch of stand-alone stories. Your class, intelligence, food love, and cool charisma were exactly what I needed to push me through to the finish line.

Aubrey Martinson at Crown, thanks for looking over my work and making a rookie author look like he kind of knows what he's doing. Most important, thanks for reining in my "awoogas."

Every athlete needs a coach, so why not a writer? My coach is Avery Rome. Avery, you taught me style and helped me find my voice. More than that, you spent hours sometimes as a therapist, other times as an interrogator, until I nailed down the meat of what I was trying to say, even if I didn't yet know it. This book would not have happened without you. Thank you.

Thanks to my hunting family. Churchie, Hunter, Dean, Tussin, and Dave Simantob. You all helped fill my life with adventures worth writing about. There's nobody I'd rather sit around the fire and talk shit to. Special thanks to Steve Rinella for having me on your *MeatEater* podcast, which kicked off this whole endeavor.

To all my favorite eating partners—Mark Priceman, Joubin Gabbay, Tiffany Gabbay, Julia Gabbayan, Natasha Gabbayan, Fara Gabbayan, Paul Feinstein, Kayvan Gabbay, Saam Gabbay, Shervin Behin, Shahram Behin, Nilou Dardashti, Josh Sarraf, Tiki Ahuja, Dan Richardson, Grant Welson, Matt Katz, Peter Davos, Omar Al-Sinjari, Mike Ghalchi, Rabindra Watson, Carole Bonnassies, Ginger Gonzaga, Will Nazar, Dave Mechlowicz, Todd Weiser, Carolyn Gross, Josh Heald, Hayden Schlossberg, Jon Hurwitz, Bret Ernst, Phil Rosenthal, Andy Gordon, Jordan Carlos, Michelle Buteau, Gijs Van Der Most, Audrey Barth, Diaa Nour, Omar Nour, Ben Schmerler, Amit Melwani, Piero Incisa, Evan Silverberg, Steve Muller, Bill Weinstein, Ilan Hall, Hamid Simantob, Dougie Cash, Lindsay Heller, Leah Kerendian, Ralph Macchio, Suzy Weiss, Abigail and Zach Schrier. Thanks for always replying "yes" to my "are you hungry?" texts.

To all the incredible chefs in my family who have made Persian food at restaurants inedible—Mom, Nahid Gabbay, Helen Gabbay (Zan Dai Joon), Khaleh Dochi, Anti Parvin, Anti Shahnaz, Anti Shahlah, Anti Yaffa, Haleh Gabbay, Shahlah Gabbay, Catherine Gabbay, Hilda Ganjian, and Noura Shabatian. Debbie Kerendian, GFY.

Nilou Nirouzi, thanks for picking me up when I was down and cheerleading me every step of the way back up. (Also, your cooking rocks my world.)

Thanks to all the restaurants through the years that have made their places feel like home: Estela, Marvin, Nanban-Kan, Turks and Frogs, Pastis, Schiller's, Balthazar, Here's Lookin' at You, Horses, Casa Mono, Salute, Bryant and Cooper, Aux Deux Amis, L'Avant Comptoir, Chez Georges.

Thanks to Traeger for being the first company to take me seriously as a food personality. I'll be forever grateful to Chad Ward, Alex Noshirvan, and the rest of the Traegerhood.

Bari Weiss and Nellie Bowles, thanks for your guidance throughout this process—even when that guidance was, "You'll do great Dan, in the meantime try this Prosecco cocktail we invented." You both give me a target as to whom I strive to be intellectually.

Sometimes you just need someone to tell you how great you

are to keep you going, and that person in my life is Matt Katz, my partner in the Verge. You're always the first person I call to share good and bad career news with, and your positive disposition makes me hang up feeling great no matter what the news was. I owe you unlimited dinners for the Avery intro.

Mohaned Al-Humadi, this book would obviously not be possible without you. Having you in my life has led to joy, laughter, introspection, and growth like I never thought possible. Thanks for letting me share our wonderfully unique relationship with the world. You're a Renaissance man whom I'm proud to call my best friend.

David Ahdoot, I wasn't born your older brother, but I hope I've grown into a decent one. Sure you might be taller, better looking, more funny, confident, but at least I—wait, I forgot where this was going. Thanks for being my North Star. You keep me ethically honest and morally sound. In other words, you my brah brah you take care care.

Finally, thanks to my parents, Rachel and Parviz Ahdoot. Mom, you taught me how to cook. Dad, you taught me how to eat. You both taught me how to be funny, work hard, and love harder. You went through catastrophe, and you still managed to be the best parents I could ever hope for. I'm nothing without you.

ABOUT THE AUTHOR

Dan Ahdoot is a stand-up comic, an actor, a writer, and a restaurateur. He's an actor on Netflix's *Cobra Kai,* Showtime's *Shameless,* Disney's *Kickin' It,* and NBCUniversal's *Bajillion Dollar Propertie$*. Dan is the host of the Food Network show *Raid the Fridge* and the host of the number one food podcast in the country, *Green Eggs and Dan*. He's also part owner of the acclaimed restaurant Estela in New York City.

ABOUT THE TYPE

This book was set in Granjon, a modern recutting of a typeface produced under the direction of George W. Jones (1860–1942), who based Granjon's design upon the letter-forms of Claude Garamond (1480–1561). The name was given to the typeface as a tribute to the typographic designer Robert Granjon (1513–89).